One
Great
Idea

Can Revolutionize Your
BUSINESS

INSIGHT PUBLISHING
SEVIERVILLE, TENNESSEE

One
Great
Idea
Can Revolutionize Your
BUSINESS

Disclaimer: This book is a compilation of ideas from numerous experts who have each contributed a chapter. As such, the views expressed in each chapter are of those who were interviewed and not necessarily of the interviewer or Insight Publishing.

Published by Insight Publishing Company
P.O. Box 4189
Sevierville, Tennessee 37864

Cover design: Emmy Shubert
Edited by: Sandra Pinkoski

10 9 8 7 6 5 4 3 2

Printed in the United States of America

ISBN-13: 978-1-60013-179-0
ISBN-10: 1-60013-179-4

Table of Contents

A Message from the Publisher

If you think this book is about only one great idea, think again! From ideas on providing great customer service to time management to getting customers and keeping them to handling troubled teens, this book has it all. As I became acquainted with what these authors had to say, I was impressed with how simple yet profound their ideas are.

As a book publisher, I've seen many different and innovative ideas. This book contains ideas I'd never even heard about before. These ideas have made a difference in the lives of those who have tried them. These ideas really work!

I continue to be amazed at the many varied and innovative ideas people can find to make their lives and businesses successful. Sometimes it takes experiencing failure to break through to success. Sometimes you have to find out how not to do something in order to find the best way to get it done. These ideas will stretch your thinking and give you a unique learning experience. The ideas inside this book will help you revolutionize your business.

Interviews conducted by:
David E. Wright
President, International Speakers Network

1

Sherry Buffington

Change Channeling:
The Fast Track to Success

The term "Change Channeling" may bring to mind sitting on the sofa and clicking through television channels, but this idea has nothing to do with television sets. This is about purposefully channeling or directing the one thing we can all count on in our lives—change. Change Channeling enables you to experience success on a more regular basis and to design your own future.

Isaac Asimov observed that the only constant is change—an astute observation that seems truer in today's world than ever before. Change is such a constant today that for many, just keeping up gets harder and harder. The increasing pace of change is a disturbing trend to many people, but not to all. Some people—those who know how to direct change so it works to their advantage—are actually benefiting from the increased pace and some even actively seek change.

The average person tries to avoid change if life is at all bearable. Even the term "Change Channeling" is disturbing to those who resist change because it requires a shift in thinking. In workshops, these resistant souls will sometimes inquire as to why one would use "change channeling" rather than "channeling change." The answer: to get your attention and make you aware of your initial reaction to change.

How did you react? Did you resist the term at first or find it an interesting twist? Does the more familiar "channeling change" feel more comfortable? Observing your response to this term will give you some insights into your approach to change. If you still feel even a little resistance after your initial response, your comfort zone may be holding you back.

People who move through life successfully are not disturbed by change. In fact, they embrace it. They recognize that change can be a positive catalyst that can move those who know how to direct it closer to their ideal. They also recognize that change can derail them and cause them to lose ground unless they manage it effectively, which they work purposefully to do. It isn't always possible to manage the external world, of course, but successful people have learned to manage their response to it in positive, beneficial, and strength-building ways.

It doesn't matter what we do or fail to do, we are either moving forward in life or we are falling behind, depending on how we approach and manage change. Successful people know that there is no standing still, there is no hiding from life's challenges, and there is no maintaining the status quo. The comfort zone is not a friend to successful people. They courageously step outside of it, determined to explore, understand, and benefit from the unknown.

At any given moment, we are either channeling change or letting change channel us. Allowing change to occur on its own is like allowing a garden to tend itself. In time all we have is weeds. Just as keeping the garden in your backyard healthy and beautiful requires attention, planning, responsible action, and the willingness to experience a little discomfort, so too does keeping your life healthy and successful. And, as with maintaining a garden, maintaining the direction and quality of your life can be both enjoyable and profitable when you take the right approach.

To ensure that the changes you make are channeled toward what you really want, learn to attend to change the same way you would attend to a beloved private garden. The ten steps listed below will help you begin doing just that. If you apply the steps faithfully, they will move you toward positive change faster and more easily than you might have ever imagined. This process will take a little work initially, but the results are often phenomenal.

Ten Steps to Creating Success through Change Channeling:

1. **Take an honest inventory of your life**. On three separate sheets of paper (preferably in a journal that you can continue to refer back to) divide your life into three categories: 1) the things that you are happy with, 2) the things that are acceptable, but not really great, and 3) the things that are just not working for you, and with which you are deeply dissatisfied.
2. **Take the third category and prioritize it**. Decide which of the things in the third category are causing you the most trouble, holding you back the most, or preventing you from being happy and successful. Once you have prioritized this list, take the top three items on the list and make a heading for each problem on three additional sheets of paper.
3. **Get really perturbed about what is not working**. As long as you accept the unsatisfactory circumstances of your life or remain resigned to them, positive change is not likely to occur. It's easy to pretend that things aren't all that bad and to look the other way, but hoping things will get better never makes them better any more than hoping that the weeds taking over your garden will magically disappear. To turn that weed-infested patch of dirt into something beautiful, the weeds are going to have to disturb you enough to move you to action. The "weeds" in this case are bad habits and situations that you have failed to deal with effectively. So take the top three items in category 3 and get really perturbed about what they are doing to your life. See these as really nasty, invasive weeds that, if left alone, will soon take over and destroy the acceptable things in category 2 and eventually damage the good things in category 1. Let the idea of these "weeds" destroying or diminishing the good things in your life concern, disturb, and perturb you to the point that you know you *must* do something about them and that you become willing to actually *do* what it takes.
4. **Discover the beliefs that have allowed these problems to exist and alter them**. Problems generally continue to exist in our lives because we have built a belief around them. We are telling ourselves a story that allows the situation to continue to exist. Before you can eliminate the problem, you must rewrite the story. Motivational expert, Anthony Robbins, devised two questions that are excellent for helping to uncover old stories, which we will use here. To uncover your stories, take each of the problems you have identified and ask yourself, "To do this (or feel this) what would I have to

believe?" When you uncover the belief, ask, "To believe this, what story would I have to be telling myself?" Write these out. You'll be amazed at how much insight this exploration will provide.

5. **Invalidate the belief and change the story**. A belief can be retained only so long as we continue to validate it by selecting criteria that gives it life. The validation criteria then become part of the story. Say, for example, that you've always wanted to start your own business, but don't believe you can ever be successful. Begin by examining the facts around that belief. How many businesses have you started and failed? None? One? Three? Most successful business owners have failed at least once, and many fail several times before finding the right formula.

The difference between those who eventually achieve success and those who quit is the stories they attach to the failure. Successful people tell themselves that the failure occurred because they don't yet have the right formula. They tell themselves they need more information or more experience and then set out to get it. Those who give up in defeat tell themselves that the failure means they are inadequate and will never be good at running a business.

Both the successful entrepreneur and the quitter had experiences of failure, but the story of the former was, "I didn't do that right. I need more information and/or experience. I will get what I need and correct my course." The story of the latter was, "I didn't do that right and that means I'm a failure. I'd better give up before I'm in so deep I can't ever dig myself out." Both faced the same situation but had completely different outcomes as a result of completely different stories.

Uncover the limiting stories you have been telling yourself. Then find *new evidence* to invalidate these old stories and begin creating new, more effective ones. Using the above example, you could begin recalling times when you succeeded at something and injecting those memories into the story of "I'm a failure." You can't maintain the "I'm a failure" story when you start invalidating it with successes you've had. The subconscious mind can hold onto a belief only so long as evidence supports it. The minute you start noticing evidence that invalidates the belief, the belief will start to fall apart. Once the subconscious mind becomes aware of criteria that invalidate the belief, it will *instantly* eliminate the belief. Once the belief is gone, so too are the actions and attitudes that were driven by it. You are then free to take new and better actions.

6. **Decide what it will take to get better outcomes**. Once you have done steps one through five you will most likely find that you feel differently about the problems you have identified. You will likely be able to see their affect more clearly and will be more determined to re-channel your energies in new, more successful directions. But some problems are such that we need to re-learn behaviors or gather new information before the problem can be fully resolved. Where this is the case, decide what *specific* changes you will need to make to eliminate the top three things you identified from category 3. List the changes on the appropriate worksheet and begin brainstorming ways to remedy each one. Get creative and stay solution focused. You have identified the problems, now focus on solutions.

7. **Create a specific, doable action plan**. Once you have spelled out what it will take to eliminate the top three problems from your life, lay out a plan for actually taking the steps. What will you do today, tomorrow, and every day until the problem is *gone?* What tools or information do you need to carry this out? How will you get them? Be sure each step is believable and doable. It's better to lay out fifteen tiny, but believable and doable steps that you can actually work on than to lay out two or three big steps that you may find too daunting to tackle.

8. **Accentuate the positive and eliminate the negative**. There's an old song lyric that advises, "Accentuate the positive, eliminate the negative . . . and don't mess with Mr. In-between." That's really good advice. When you accentuate the positive, you are focusing on the things you want to grow (category 1). And the interesting thing is that's exactly what we do—grow what we focus on. In eliminating the negative, you are working on your category 3 items to eliminate them and you eliminate them most easily by *accentuating the positive*. By telling yourself positive stories in relation to the category 3 items as well as drawing on the positive proofs from category 1 to invalidate category 3 items, you can effectively *eliminate the negative*. "Mr. In-between" represents the category 2 items. They are neither good nor bad so you don't need to waste your energy on these. As the negative items are eliminated, the in-between items will either improve and move into the positive category or they will remain mildly satisfactory and will not cause any

problems. Don't waste any energy on "Mr. In-between" unless the things in category 2 move to category 3.

9. **Take action**. Once you have uncovered the beliefs that have kept the problems alive and have begun to rewrite the stories connected to them, begin taking the specific steps you outlined in your plan. Nothing will propel you forward faster than the experience of success, and each time you take one of those small, doable steps and succeed, your success stories grow and are better validated. It's true that nothing succeeds like success.

10. **Repeat the process of elimination until category 3 disappears**. You'll discover that once you have eliminated the top three items in category 3, the other items in that category are a cinch to eliminate. And once all those problematic habits and beliefs are gone, life begins to flow, beautifully unencumbered. You will find you are more in control of the changes that occur in your life and you are better able to channel them toward success on every level.

With the dawning of each new day you have the opportunity to decide how your day and ultimately your life will unfold. What you choose will determine whether you create a beautiful landscape or contend with nasty weeds that choke out your potential and obscure your charm. Choose the beautiful landscape. You're worth it!

Meet Sherry Buffington...

DR. SHERRY BUFFINGTON has been immersed in the study of human nature, motivation, change, and success principles since 1982. She is founder and director of NaviCore International, a research and development firm focused on human personality, development, motivation, and effectiveness. Dr. Buffington is a pioneer in the field of personality and developmental assessments. She is the originator of the highly acclaimed *CORE Multidimensional Awareness Profile* and *CORE Personal Effectiveness Profile.* She is a psychologist, trainer, coach, and author who has authored and co-authored several books, including *Who's Got the Compass? . . . I Think I'm Lost!* Her work has taken assessments to a whole new level and her dedication to understanding and improving the human condition has contributed to the transformation of hundreds of organizations and thousands of individual lives and relationships.

Sherry Buffington
NaviCore International, Inc.
Phone: 214.688.1412 or outside Texas, toll-free: 877.884.2673
E-mail: sherry@navicoreinternational.com
www.navicoreinternational.com

2

Stan Craig

Great ideas need landing gears as well as wings.
—O. C. Jackson

Every business needs one thing to survive—customers. Once you have them, other things will become important; but without customers little else matters.

My wife and I just returned from Germany. We visited a small village along the Rhine that was famous for its museum of music boxes with mechanical movements. Nearby were charming local shops selling beautiful and intricate mechanical music boxes with movement and music. When we returned home after weeks of being away, my wife began sorting and reviewing the catalogues she had received while we were gone. There, on the last pages of a beautiful catalogue, were the exact same music boxes we had so admired in Germany.

In a world where nearly every service is being offered and every product is available at every turn, getting customers has never been more challenging.

You picked up this book looking for one great idea. But most of you readers already have a great idea; you have a business or service you offer and you want to put it to work more effectively. Often it is not a lack of ideas slowing us down—it is the inability to find the right landing gear to put the ideas to work. Every great idea needs landing gear—a way for that great idea to come back to earth.

The landing gear for most businesses today is finding customers in a world full of duplication and competition. How do you compete to get the right customers and, more importantly, turn one customer or client into 10 or 20 or 100 or 1000?

I'm going to share with you one great idea—a landing gear to systematically grow your business by finding new clients.

Nearly every business book written in the last 10 years talks about the importance of WOM, or word-of-mouth. From Seth Godin's terrific book, <u>The Idea Virus</u>, to Malcolm Gladwell's, <u>The Tipping</u>

Point, the value of word-of-mouth marketing has been made extremely clear. But where is the landing gear? We know we need WOM, but how do we create word-of-mouth marketing in a simple easily-remembered way that can grow our business?

Here's the idea and, like all ideas, it is simply a revision of a previous idea. I learned as a beginning financial consultant that getting recommendations from a current client is the best way to get new business, but I couldn't figure out how to make getting referrals comfortable enough to make it a daily habit. The number one objection to asking for referrals is the fear of appearing to be in need. Everyone wants to appear successful. Too many have the idea that "if I ask for a referral I'm obviously not successful." That is the wrong conclusion but it is based upon a very valid observation: Most people do not like to give referrals and, outside of the sales profession, are not familiar or comfortable with the word "referral".

The idea that changed my approach and resulted in a steady stream of new clients was taught to me by my good friend Larry Biederman. Larry had the same problem as every salesman: how to get new business. As a former tennis professional, teacher and coach he had often asked for advice and found that he was never refused. So when he became a financial consultant, asking for advice was a simple and easy way to grow his financial services business. His success was outstanding. He was promoted to the highest levels of his firm and at every level he practiced and taught this process. I learned it a long time ago and I'm happy to pass a simplified version on to you. It truly is one great idea. Apply it to your business and discover just how effective it can be in making your own great idea successful.

When you are with any client or customer, this approach will help you comfortably get all the referrals you can possibly work with.

Your question—

"Mr. or Ms._____, do you have a few minutes to give me some advice?"

Nearly every time, the client's response is,
"Sure, what about?"

Your thoughtful reply-
"I would like to grow my (_____) business by working with more successful (doctors, lawyers, businessmen, farmers, dentists, real estate agents, people in your neighborhood, members of your club, etc.) just like you. Do you think that's a good idea?"

The client's usual response-

"Sure."

The next significant question can change your business overnight: "If you were me, how would you do it?"

Now here's the hardest part for any one in sales no matter the product: shut up. Most everyone I know who is selling anything is nervous about the process and that nervousness often translates into excess conversation. I'm convinced that more people talk themselves out of business by not knowing when to be quiet than by saying too little.

If you will just listen, your client will explain to you exactly how to get in touch with the people you want to meet: other successful individuals just like them. Once you put the system into practice you will be amazed at the smart, innovative and successful ways your clients will give you to meet more new prospects than you would have ever found on your own.

There may be an occasion when a client will respond with a "no" or "I'm not sure" to your question, "Do you think that is a good idea?" Your reply then is...

"Oh, why do you say that?"

Then listen.

The reply is usually that their acquaintances are all taken care of or they have probably already been approached. Your reply is...

"I don't want to interfere with anyone's relationships but most people like having choices. More choices can confirm or inform and I am happy to help with either... who do you think I should be talking to?"

This is the landing gear to get the customers to put your own idea to work: ask for their advice. Every time you ask someone for advice you are giving him or her a complement. You're suggesting that they are important, knowledgeable and caring. This is light years away from asking for referrals. And when you ask for their advice you are much more likely to reach more successful individuals just like them. And believe me, what they will tell you can provide more help and assistance than you ever dreamed.

This approach adds a second element to successful marketing— niche marketing.

A successful business knows its niche market and strives to lead in that market. By asking for advice you are making a conscious effort to duplicate your best clients—the clients you enjoy working with, the clients who will help you become more successful as you help them. These are the very clients who will provide the tools and the ideas to successfully grow your business in their niche.

For over 10 years PSB has trained thousands in using this process. PSB Training offers seminars on how the advice process can be used as a part of every sales professional's approach to growing his or her business. There are a number of aspects of this approach to be learned but the fundamental idea is the advice process.

Try it for yourself. Stop asking for referrals and start asking for advice. You will find the landing gear to get all the right kind of clients you need to grow your successful business.

STAN CRAIG is a successful entrepreneur, speaker, writer and consultant with over thirty years experience in sales and marketing. He is a partner in PSB Training as well as being the principal in his own firm, Legacy Leadership. A member of the National Speaker's Association, Stan offers keynote speeches as well as training sessions and seminars to a wide variety of clients. His clients include Merrill Lynch, Citigroup, Wachovia Bank, Nationwide Insurance, UBS and nearly every other financial firm on Wall Street. He also consults for online marketing with such firms as TD Ameritrade and FOLIOfn.

His "Four Biblical Roles of Leadership" and "Plain Talk on Selling", along with PSBs Advice process—"Smart Marketing"—are among his most requested presentations. The motivational keynote, "The 5-Pointed Compass" is a personal journey that inspires and renews audiences with the 5 distinct points to unusual success. Stan is co-author with Allen Keys, Warren Bennis and others of the Book, *Leadership Defined*.

He may be reached at stan@stancraig.com or stan@psbtraining.com. You may also call 910-540-1447. Stan lives with his wife, Gloria, in Southport, NC, and Louisville, KY. He is available for any size meeting or conference. For more information see his website www.stancraig.com. He is also a member of the International Speaker's Network and may be booked by calling

Brenda Keefer
International Speakers Network & Insight Publishing
647 Wall Street
Sevierville, TN 37862
Phone: 800.987.7771
Fax: 865.429.4523
www.isnworks.com

Carri Kenning
PSB Training
For 450 Tilton Road, Suite 942
Northfield NJ spacebar 08225
phone: 609 484 3200

3

Toni Henderson-Mayers

The Job Alternative

I remember being approached by a previous student who really needed a jumpstart in her career. She, like many, was tired of working from nine to five. She was tired of the everyday routine of "business as usual." She was tired of commuting one hour to work and one hour back home each night. She was tired of the stress of rushing without a single minute to console her crying child as she dropped her off at daycare. She was tired of pressing her way to work through snow, sleet, and rain only to battle an over demanding supervisor. She was simply, tired.

Many of us, like this student, are really suffering in our careers, whether it is our mundane schedules, the commute to work, or a lack of passion in what we do.

Consider the following advice and job alternatives to breathe new life into your career and ultimately your whole life.

Find the Passion

I'm sure you have heard more than your share of "Find Your Passion" or "Live Your Passion" speeches or topics, but it really is important. It is amazing to me the amount of time and effort many have placed into careers they care nothing about. It is only a matter of time before this person is "burned out" and wants to quit the work he or she is doing. You must like what you are doing, be excited about doing it, and of course over time be paid well for doing it.

If you have not done a thorough "soul-searching," please take the time now to do the following exercise: Write down on a blank sheet of paper five hobbies, activities, or odd jobs you would do for free. Is there something you would do even if you were awakened at three in the morning to do it? If so, write it down. In another list of five, write down what you are good at or what others have said you are good at. Lastly, write a note to yourself on the back of that sheet of paper about what you envision yourself doing. No doubt throughout your life you have been given "hunches" about what you should be doing with your life. When you dream, what do you see? What are you wearing? Where are you living? What types of people are you talking to? What are you doing?

Once completed, take some time to go over this exercise. Do you notice some similar themes about you that are coming across? Does a certain hobby or pastime keep popping up? In the "vision" exercise, does your life match up to what you see? If not, why not slowly but surely change things in your current life to reflect what you see in your future life?

Each small step you take to live a life of passion and purpose will lead you closer to the career that was meant for you. But what does this all have to do with "The Job Alternative"? Well, many are caught in the same scenario as my previous student. They get caught up in lives and careers they absolutely hate. How? There are many, many reasons, but one major reason for sure is they forget to follow their passion.

Now that you know what your passion is, let's look into alternatives to the nine-to-five job.

Telecommuting

Telecommuting, a term coined by Jack Nilles and first used in the United States, involves the ability to be flexible in one's schedule by working from home as well as at the office. This is accomplished by making prior arrangements with one's employer to work a few days at the "head" office and a few days from one's home. To be successful in this venture, you need to have all the necessary office equipment to get your job done. This may include a phone, fax machine or service, computer, cell phone, e-mail, copier, and whatever else it would take to get the job done.

Telecommuting works great for those who want freedom from the tight nine-to-five constraints, but who want some structure or routine to their day. It is also a great launching pad for those considering starting their own business since it gives an opportunity to set flexible hours and individualized goals for achieving success. You can test out what it may be like to "run your own show," if you will.

Setting up a telecommuting deal with your employer is more likely when you have worked for the company awhile and have proven yourself as a valuable employee. Recently, however, there have been many opportunities for telecommuting positions as companies have embraced the idea more readily. Many companies are designing their new positions to incorporate telecommuting. Searching for an opportunity to telecommute is not as difficult as it once was.

I was fortunate in one of my last "traditional" positions to be able to telecommute. Two to three times a week I would come into the office for meetings, conduct interviews, or speak with my staff. After a few hours I would travel to meet with clients. On the days I worked from home I would catch up on reports, make phone calls, and set appointments. It was wonderful and it allowed me to spend a great deal of time with my then, two-year-old.

Work from Home

Working from home is very similar to having a home-based business except it usually alludes to working for someone else, but from your home. Usually this opportunity is available through some company because of a need to have a task completed or a service rendered.

The key here is to research the company and opportunity thoroughly and to ask for references. There are so many scams and one has to be careful. If it sounds too good to be true, it probably is.

Many friends and acquaintances of mine have been duped by opportunities to stuff envelopes, assemble products, or fill out surveys. Don't let this be you! There may be some companies that offer many of the same opportunities and be legit. Just look into the offer thoroughly. Get a good understanding of what your duties are and how you will be paid. I suggest getting the agreement in writing and having a lawyer look it over. Personally, I have not worked any "work from home" opportunities because many of the companies did not pass my closer inspection.

Home-Based Business

A home-based business is simply a business you run from home. It can be any type of business from babysitting to an online store front. Typically if you have a computer, phone, and fax or fax service, you can be in business. If you had the opportunity, what type of business would you start? Can it possibly be run from home?

Businesses such as day care services, plumbers, online computer work, trainers, clowns, Web site designer, independent sales representative, and the list goes on, can all be done from home. Some businesses can be run from inside the home and/or the home can be used for office functions and the actual services can be performed outside the home.

A dear friend of mine is a corporate trainer who does all of her paperwork, phone calls, and other necessary office procedures from her home office. When it comes time to train, she goes to her clients and performs training services. Plumbers, electricians, clowns, and massage therapists tend to run their businesses in this way.

There are many who sell items from their Web sites and maintain those business transactions from home. This type of service does not require the owner to go outside of the home but rather complete all office procedures from the comfort of his or her home. Businesses like these are growing and no one is the wiser that you may have a budding empire with its headquarters in your garage.

Independent Contractor

As an independent contractor you as an individual or your business can contract products or services to another business or entity. You are not an employee; but rather, a company doing business with another company. Most independent contractors establish themselves as corporations or limited liability companies. Speak to your certified pubic accountant for more information.

Being an independent contractor has been the most enjoyable for me because it allows me the opportunity to run my business the way I like, set my own hours, and decide when and where I would like to work. All of my speaking engagements and most of my training services are handled through independent contracting.

Is it possible that your services can be contracted out as well? Nurses, case workers, recruiters, therapists, performers, and the like have contracted their services. If you want to own your own business and have the freedom to schedule your next work project and decide when and where it will begin, independent contracting may be for you.

Multiple Career Centers

Through the years I have helped thousands find jobs, careers they were excited about, and turn their lives around. In that time, I went from helping people find jobs to finding their "calling" in life. For some that calling led them to start businesses of their own. For others, the thought of starting a business seemed too big of a task to undertake. Because of this, I developed a concept I call, "Multiple Career Centers."

The Multiple Career Centers concept consists of three to five small streams of income where the total is equal to or is more than your monthly expenses. In other words, if you need $1,000 a month to run your household and to make sure all your monthly expenses are paid, you will need to set up multiple career centers that will total $1,000 or more in profits. So let's say you had four multiple career centers, each center would need to make a profit of $250 or more each month.

I have found that doing business this way has seemed more obtainable for many and it also takes the fear away of owning a business. If coached correctly, you too can have a multiple career center. This system is quite unique and has only been offered to my clients. If you have a few hobbies or a few ideas that can profit even a small amount each month, multiple career centers may be for you.

So you see, if you are tired of the nine-to-five daily grind, there is no reason why you can't find a job alternative.

Meet Toni Henderson-Mayers...

TONI MAYERS brings over twenty years of experience in careers, business, and entrepreneurship. She is a sought-after speaker whose message encourages us all to find careers and relationships we are "excited about" and look for passion in our lives. She is the host of the podcast, "The Job Alternative," which can be accessed through iTunes or on her Web site. This show features various types of career opportunities from working from nine to five, operating a home-based business, or setting up various streams of income. Toni is a member of the National Speakers Association.

Toni Henderson-Mayers
Go Toni Network
P.O. Box 939
Hope Mills, NC 28348
Phone: 877.511.0800 Hotline and fax
E-mail: info@gotoni.org
www.gotoni.org

4

Deborah Faithrose

Eddie's Story

The year was 2000—a new century, a new millennium. It was an exciting time to be alive. But for me, it was one of the most challenging and traumatic times of my life. I sat waiting to be called for jury duty with a feeling of despair as every part of my life seemed to be broken. I was chosen along with a few other potential jurors to leave the courthouse and travel by bus to another location. We were relocated to the county juvenile justice alternative school where a case involving one of the students was unfolding and could possibly go to court.

We were led into a conference room to sit and wait. As people began to read newspapers, make calls to their office, or make conversation with each other, I began to hear another conversation outside the conference room. It was coming from the counselor's office across the hall.

A decision was being made about one of the students. Should he be given a second chance at the school or should he be moved to a high security location—juvenile jail? The voices in the counselor's office expressed pros and cons regarding the boy's fate. The life of the fifteen-year-old boy unfolded as the debate continued.

There was the argument for giving him a second chance. After all, imagine living in his situation for fifteen years: At the age of three, his parents gave him to his grandparents. The grandparents passed him off to an aunt. From there, he had a short stay with cousins. Two years later, he was passed back to his parents who were not at all happy about his return. By the age of five, he had been shuffled around like an unwanted puppy. Between the ages of eight to ten, he had been in and out of emergency rooms for injuries caused by physical abuse at home. The house rule was to stay in his room and not to speak.

By the age of fifteen, he had experienced rejection, abuse, and oppression. These were the reasons being presented in favor of giving him a second chance. And yet, the debate began to lean in favor of incarceration based on the same reasons.

The boy's life hanging in limbo drew my thoughts away from my own life as I hoped for his second chance. A feeling of sympathetic connection to the plight of this fifteen-year-old teen in trouble filled my heart. Finally, a voice spoke up with a decision. He was considered dangerous to the other students and teachers. The boy would be incarcerated. My heart sank. Even though logic told me that I didn't know what he had done to deserve this fate, still I felt sympathy and said a silent prayer for this faceless, nameless teenager whom I would never meet.

I tried to focus on the noise in the room filled with potential jurors. But the conversation I had just heard sent my thoughts in a different direction. It made me wish I could do something to help the kids in this school. But could I really do anything that would make a difference when my own life was in such a mess?

I remembered the "Youth Leadership Program" that Toastmasters International offered. Toastmasters is an organization for people who want to speak more effectively. Since this program is designed to help young people develop their leadership qualities through learning communication skills, this would be an excellent project for students at this school. Most youth leadership coordinators promoted the program to exemplary students in schools, churches, and communities to teenagers who show promise for success in their future.

I began to think of the kids who have trauma and challenge in their life just as I was having. What about them? Why not them? What if they have leadership potential but without opportunity to express it or without anyone to encourage that expression?

Why not present a Youth Leadership Program to teens who truly need and deserve someone to believe they can be leaders? So the idea was born to give the program to teens at the county juvenile justice alternative school.

My friends thought I was crazy. They said, "You have no experience with teens that are exemplary, much less teens that are in trouble." But it seemed this idea had been divinely inspired and I knew I had to do it.

First, I needed to create a lesson plan that would pass the scrutiny of the school's board of directors. The plan was presented and approved. I was given twenty students who all volunteered, mainly out of curiosity and to get out of other classes for an hour. Nonetheless, they did volunteer for whatever reason. I was told the last boy to volunteer would be trouble. In fact, he was almost not allowed to participate. His name was Eddie.

I thought I was to be the teacher and this would be my story. Fortunately, I was wrong. Eddie was the teacher and the story became Eddie's story. Eddie sat in the back of the room on the first day and every day of the eight-week program. Even though he was in the back, he made his presence known.

During the second class, the students began to deliver prepared speeches. The objective was to stand up in front of the class and share their thoughts, feelings, and hopes through personal stories. The students were doing surprisingly well as they slowly began to trust enough to share their life experiences. As each student had the courage to stand up in front of the class to speak, Eddie interrupted with rude heckling.

I noticed a pattern in Eddie's heckling. His interruptions were placed precisely as the speaker began to relate stories of hardship. It was as if Eddie were shielding himself from hearing painful details. On the outside it made him appear tough and unemotional.

Trying to lessen Eddie's behavior was futile. In fact, any attempt to stop his behavior served as fuel to make his comments louder. I began to understand why my friends had warned me about getting involved with these teens. What had I gotten myself into?

All the students had completed their first speaking assignment— all except for Eddie. Before he agreed to come to the front and speak, he said, "Miss Deborah, on the first day of class, you promised we could speak on any topic we wanted. Now Miss Deborah, was that the truth or was it a lie to get us to talk?"

I said, "Eddie, the moment you are in front of your audience, the floor is yours to speak as you wish on any topic. You can express any feeling, emotion, or opinion you want and we will listen."

Eddie replied, "Okay Miss Deborah, I'm ready to give my speech." He swaggered from the back of the room looking tough and unconcerned. His speech began with, "I'm gonna tell all of you like it is in my house. In my house I do whatever I want to do because I can. So this speech and every speech will be about my favorite topic—sex."

He paused, turned to look at me as if daring me to go back on my word in front of the class. I swallowed hard and forced myself to say, "Please, continue your speech."

He proceeded to use offensive language as he described in detail his activities after school with his many girlfriends. Each sentence ended with "because I can." After every few words, he glanced at me as if he were expecting me to go back on my word and interrupt his speech or reprimand him. I knew that would only validate his distrust.

As he continued to speak, even the students in class who thought they had seen it all and done it all became disgusted with Eddie's stories. When his language got out of hand, the student serving in the role of Master of Ceremony learned how to intervene and give him a choice to change his language or sit down. During each speech he gave, he always chose to sit down before he would change his language. His classmates were learning how to take charge and be leaders when necessary. After all, this was the purpose of the program—to allow the students to make decisions for themselves and follow through with those decisions.

As weeks passed, the students learned to trust and believe in their own abilities. They faced their fears of speaking in front of their peers. Their anger slipped away as they learned to laugh with each other. They became leaders—all except for Eddie.

During the first seven weeks, Eddie ended every speech with these words, "I talked about my favorite topic, sex, because I can."

We were quickly approaching the eighth and final week of the course. The last class was to be a celebration with awards and recognition. The students took charge of planning the celebration. For the first time in a long time (maybe the first time ever) they felt good about themselves—all except for Eddie.

The class voted to hold a speech contest for their celebration. The contest would be held in the room for special activities. Parents were invited. Administrators and board members were invited. Certificates of completion would be presented and trophies for speech contest winners would be awarded. All students would participate with a two-minute speech.

Eddie blatantly announced that he did not vote in favor of a contest and would not participate unless, as always, he could choose his own topic. He turned to me and said, "And I guess that's up to you Miss Deborah." He stared directly at me with a half grin as if to say, "Now what are you going to do?"

What *was* I going to do? In a moment of panic, I pictured Eddie standing at the microphone in front of parents, administrators, and board members giving one of his usual speeches in graphic detail about his favorite topic.

Finally, I said, "Eddie, you are wrong. It's no longer up to me. It's up to your fellow classmates." An emergency business meeting was immediately called to order. The purpose of the eight-week course was reviewed as follows: to allow each student to serve in all capacities of leadership roles, to learn Robert's Rules of Order, and to learn communication skills by giving speeches on a topic of the speaker's choice.

A motion was made to allow Eddie the freedom to speak on any topic. A heated debate ensued among the students. They were able to experience using Roberts Rules of Order for a very real situation with an outcome that would greatly affect their day of celebration. There were debates on the pros and cons as Eddie sat in the back of the room seeming to take pleasure in causing conflict. Then finally, the vote. It was close, but Eddie won his freedom of speech.

The week before the big day of celebration, I heard the students asking Eddie not to talk on his "favorite topic." And I heard his response, "What part of Robert's Rules of Order do you not understand?"

The celebration day came. The room had been decorated by the students. The table in front of the room was filled with certificates and trophies. I could feel the excitement among the students. They were nervous but with a new sense of confidence. The room began to fill up with parents, administrators, and board members.

There were different speeches with different stories to tell but the students and I had one concern in common. Would he or wouldn't he? Would Eddie give a speech on his favorite topic "because he could" and embarrass the other students and ruin future possibilities of this program ever being presented in this school or any other school?

All the students were seated at a special guest of honor table in the middle of the room. One by one the students stood up and gave their two-minute speech that ended with applause by proud family members and school officials. True to form, Eddie wanted to be last.

Finally, every student had given their speech except for Eddie. It was his turn. He swaggered to the microphone. My heart was racing; my palms were sweating as I glanced at the other students. They were all looking at him as if begging, "Please don't do it."

He stood in front of the microphone in silence for a moment which seemed like eternity. Then he began. "Miss Deborah and the other students in this class took a vote and said I could speak on any topic I wanted to. So I'm going to tell you how it is in my house."

He looked down at a piece of paper on the lectern, took a quick glance up at the audience, and then paused as if making a final decision. The room was so quiet you could hear the absence of breathing as he began his speech.

"When I was three years old, my parents gave me away to my grandparents. Then my grandparents gave me to my aunt. Then she gave me to my cousin . . ."

There was a look of extreme relief on the faces of the other students but for me there was shock and disbelief. How could it be? Could this be the same boy whose fate I had heard unfolding three months ago as I waited for jury duty? How was he able to stay in the school and how did he end up in my class, in the Youth Leadership Program? My mind was spinning with questions as Eddie continued his story. He related that he didn't remember how he ended up back at his parents' house but he remembered they didn't want him there. He remembered how he stayed in his room and was forbidden to speak or express feelings.

The more he spoke, the more I knew it was him. My eyes filled with tears. Over the course of three months, a miracle had happened. Eddie continued his story of his home being filled with anger and physical violence. At the end of his speech, he said, "And to the people at this school who let me stay, gave me a second chance, and let me go to Miss Deborah's speech class, I want to thank you, because I can."

As he returned to his seat, his classmates spontaneously rose from their seats in tremendous applause. From his seat, he looked up at his audience still standing and applauding. For the first time he expressed gratitude with a genuine smile. And for the first time, I saw the real Eddie. Needless to say, he was awarded the first-place trophy which was the first positive recognition he had ever received in his fifteen years of life.

As the celebration came to a close and we hugged and said our goodbyes, I knew that all along, Eddie had been the teacher and it was Eddie's story.

On that day, he taught me one great lesson. Eddie taught me how deeply human it is to express emotions, thoughts, and ideas and how deeply wrong it is to have that taken away.

The one great idea that I share with you, I learned from Eddie. The greatest gift you can give another is the gift of freedom to express. Give the gift to co-workers and employees. Give the gift to friends and family. Most importantly, give it to yourself.

So to you, Eddie, I say, "Thank you 'because I can.' "

Meet Deborah Faithrose...

DEBORAH FAITHROSE brings more than fifteen years of experience in professional speaking and training to audiences around the country. She teaches life by touching hearts. She has received awards for her entertaining presentations both in the realm of comedy and inspiration. Deborah is certified in Hypno-Coaching,™ Handwriting Analysis, and Master of Ceremony Protocol. She is affiliated with Toastmasters International, National Guild of Hypnotists, National Federation of Neuro-Linguistic Psychology, and International Association of Counselors and Therapists.

Deborah Faithrose, CH, CI
Faithrose Seminars
3767 Forest Lane, Ste124, #1220
Dallas, TX 75244
Phone: 866-620-7673
Fax: 972-620-2210
E-mail: dfaithrose@sbcglobal.net
www.deborahfaithrose.com

5

Bud Bilanich
"The Common Sense Guy"

Branding by Blogging

I was thrilled to be asked to contribute to *One Great Idea!* I accepted immediately. Then reality set in as I asked myself, "What is my one great idea?" I had to think about this one for a while. All of a sudden it became obvious—branding by blogging.

As a small business owner, I have long recognized the importance of branding. As a small business owner whose brand is me, I have recognized the importance of personal branding. I am a keynote speaker, executive coach, organization effectiveness consultant, and author. I am my business; therefore, my brand needs to speak for me.

When I decided that I needed to brand myself, I began by asking everybody I know a simple question: "When you think of me, what is the first thing that comes to mind?" An overwhelming number of people said, "Your commonsense approach to business and life." My first reaction was, "Uh oh, common sense doesn't make for much of a brand." Then I started to think about it a little more.

I'd read several very interesting books about personal branding. The best is *Career Distinction: Stand Out by Building Your Brand,* by William Arruda and Kirsten Dixson. *Be Your Own Brand*, by David McNally and Karl Speak; *The Brand You 50*, by Tom Peters; and *The Personal Branding Phenomenon* and *The Brand Called You*, both by Peter Montoya are also helpful books on personal branding. I also read several interesting e-books by William Arruda: *1–2–3 Success!*, *1–2–3 Success! for Coaches, 1–2–3 Success! for Entrepreneurs,* and *The Brand Discovery Workbook.*

A few things stood out in my reading:

- An effective personal brand is authentic—it reflects the true character of the individual being branded.
- An effective personal brand repels as many people as it attracts.

- An effective personal brand is consistent.

As I started thinking about what my friends and clients said, and combined their comments with what I'd learned about personal branding from my research, I began to get comfortable with common sense as the driver for my brand.

Common sense met the three tests:

Authenticity—From what people told me, and what I believe about myself, common sense is an authentic representation of who I am.

Attract/Repel—Most of my clients tell me they chose me because of my down-to-earth, commonsense style, and approach. On the other hand, I have lost business because some prospective clients decided that my commonsense approach was not "heady" enough for them and their organizational culture.

Consistency—As Popeye says, "I yam what I yam." I don't change my style to try to please a prospective client. I present myself as someone who can help clients with their needs by helping them figure out and apply commonsense solutions.

So, common sense was emerging as the theme of my brand. However, I was still unsure of a tag line for my brand. I experimented with a few things. "Common Sense Coach" was too narrow. I do things other than coaching. "Common Sense Guru" sounded too pompous and New Age all at once. "Common Sense Doctor" (a play on my educational credentials) sounded too much like a medical doctor, etc.

One day I was having a conversation about my brand tag line dilemma with a friend. I was lamenting the fact that I couldn't come up with a good tag line. I said something like, "There's this guy who calls himself 'The Goals Guy,' I wish I had enough guts to call myself 'The Common Sense Guy.'" She said, "What's wrong with 'The Common Sense Guy'?"

I hemmed and hawed and said things like, "It's kind of pedestrian; it's too informal; there's already a goals guy." As I heard myself speaking, I realized I was rationalizing. I have often said to people who were impressed with something I'd done—graduated from Harvard, started a business, written a book—"I'm just a guy." And, I had already established that I approach my work in a commonsense manner. So why not become The Common Sense Guy?

First, I trademarked "The Common Sense Guy." Then I went to the Colorado Department of Revenue and registered "Common Sense Guy" as a trade name. I redid my www.BudBilanich.com Web site. I added a section called "Personal Characteristics." I listed some words to describe me: Common Sense headed the list, followed by Cancer

Survivor, Sports Fan, Optimist, Books and Movies, Rugby, Bicycling, The Power of One. I had taken the first step in branding myself as The Common Sense Guy.

My Common Sense Guy brand met the first two of the three tests—it was authentic and it was likely to repel some people while attracting others. I felt comfortable with it. It captured what I'm all about. It resonated with most, but not all, people. I figured I was onto something good. Now I just needed to figure out how to meet the third test—consistency.

I began with my books. I have published six books. The last four all have references to common sense on the cover or in the title. For example: The cover of *4 Secrets of High Performing Organizations,* has the teaser *Common Sense, Uncommon Wisdom; Fixing Performance Problems* is subtitled *Common Sense Ideas That Work; Solving Performance Problems* (a "Walk the Talk" Handbook) is subtitled *A Common Sense Guide for Leaders at all Levels; Leading With Values* (another Walk the Talk Handbook) is subtitled *Eight Common Sense Leadership Strategies for Bringing Organizational Values to Life.* My seventh book, *Straight Talk for Success: Common Sense Ideas That Won't Let You Down,* will be out in early 2008.

My business cards and stationary say:

Bud Bilanich
The Common Sense Guy
"Common sense solutions to tough business problems"

I have several Web sites: www.BudBilanich.com is my flagship site. It tells visitors everything they could possibly want to know about me; www.CommonSenseKeynotes.com is my keynote speaker Web site; www.CommonSenseCoach.com is my executive coaching Web site; www.LeadershipCommonSense.com is a deep content site that contains all of the leadership articles I have written. My blogs, www.CommonSenseGuy.com and www.SuccessCommonSense.com, help me reinforce my commonsense message every day.

My www.CommonSenseGuy.com site has really helped me promote myself and my Common Sense Guy brand. One way I promote my commonsense brand on the blog is simple: at the end of most of my posts I begin a paragraph with the following words, "So the commonsense point here is . . ." Then I go on to explicitly state the commonsense idea behind the post.

When I began www.CommonSenseGuy.com, I described it as "a blog devoted to building a great career, leading people, and running a small business." I have done a pretty good job of maintaining these three foci.

However, recently I decided that I could do a better and more focused job by splitting off my career advice and creating a new blog, while keeping www.CommonSenseGuy.com focused on leadership and running a small business. I created a new blog to highlight my career and life success thinking and to promote my coaching business: www.SuccessCommonSense.com. I used this blog as the early content for my new book: *Straight Talk for Success.*

The www.SuccessCommonSense.com site is very focused. The model on which it is based has five points:

1. Self-confidence
2. Personal Impact
3. Outstanding Performance
4. Communication Skills
5. Interpersonal Competence

I post an article about one of these categories every day on this blog. Monday is self-confidence day, Tuesday is personal impact day, Wednesday, outstanding performance, Thursday, communication skills, and Friday is interpersonal competence. In this way I have been able to accomplish two things: I reinforce my common sense brand and I reinforce the ideas in my *Straight Talk* book.

By always posting on one subject every day, I provide readers with a simple, easy way to locate information of interest to them.

I haven't forgotten www.CommonSenseGuy.com. In fact, I have sharpened its focus too. In *4 Secrets of High Performing Organizations,* I lay out four fundamentals for running a business and leading people:

1. Establish and clearly communicate *clarity* of purpose and direction.
2. Enlist the sincere *commitment* of everyone in an organization.
3. Skillfully *execute* the things that matter.
4. Build mutually beneficial *relationships* with important outside constituencies.

This clarity, commitment, execution, relationships model is the basis of my consulting work. I use it as a diagnostic tool as well as a way to structure interventions.

Blogging has helped me gain an international reputation and build my Common Sense Guy brand. I've received comments on my blog posts from people in the United States, Latin America, Europe, Asia, and Australia (I'm still waiting for the first comment from Africa). I've booked speaking, coaching, and consulting engagements as a result of my blogging. People send me their books to review on my blogs. Other people have requested my books to review on their blogs. I receive calls to appear as a teleseminar guest. I had to open a merchant account to accept credit cards because I began getting orders for my books. I raised over $2,500 for the Alex's Lemonade Stand Foundation. I've made new friends and developed new partnerships—all as a result of my blogs.

So my "one great idea" is branding by blogging. Anyone in business needs a solid brand and mine is the Common Sense Guy. However, having a well thought-out brand is not enough. All brands need exposure. Blogging is the best way I know to get that type of exposure.

Meet Bud Bilanich...

BUD BILANICH'S pragmatic approach to business, life, and the business of life has earned him the title The Common Sense Guy and made him one of the most sought-after speakers, consultants, and executive coaches in the United States! Dr. Bilanich's work focuses on improving the performance of individuals, teams, and entire organizations. Bud is Harvard educated, but has a no-nonsense, commonsense approach to his work that stretches back to his roots in the steel country of Western Pennsylvania. His consulting and coaching clients report that he is full of practical, useful commonsense advice that they can put to work immediately. Audiences leave his commonsense keynotes armed with fundamentally sound, commonsense ideas and the motivation to put those ideas to work. Bud has thirty years of experience in the organization effectiveness field. He has worked with clients in the United States, Canada, Latin America, Europe, Australia, and Asia. His clients include Pfizer Inc, Johnson & Johnson, Abbott Laboratories, Schein Pharmaceuticals, General Motors, Citicorp, JP Morgan Chase, AT&T, Pitney Bowes, Dana Corporation, and The Boys and Girls Clubs of America.

He is the author of six books: *Fixing Performance Problems: Common Sense Ideas That Work, Four Secrets of High Performing Organizations, Leading With Values, Using Values To Turn Vision Into Reality, Solving Performance Problems: A Common Sense Guide for Leaders at all Levels, and Supervisory Leadership*. Dr. Bilanich received an EdD from Harvard University with a concentration in Organizational Behavior and Intervention. He also holds an MA in Organizational and Interpersonal Communication from the University of Colorado, and a BS in Human Development from Penn State. Bud is a cancer survivor and lives in Denver, Colorado, with Cathy, his wife. He is a retired rugby player, an avid cyclist, and a film, live theatre, and crime fiction buff.

Bud Bilanich
The Common Sense Guy
875 South Colorado Boulevard, Suite 773
Denver, CO 80246
Phone: 303.393.0446
E-mail: Bud@BudBilanich.com
www.BudBilanich.com
Blog: www.CommonSenseGuy.com, Blog: www.SuccessCommonSense.com

6

Brent Patmos

Throw Away the Resume:
The Importance of Sales Selection

In order to select the right salesperson for your next position, let me propose that you throw away the traditional dependence on candidates' resumes and focus instead on objective evidence showing you if they can sell, how they sell, and why they sell. In other words, prioritize the candidates' sales behaviors and motivators in the sales selection process. Why? Because traditional sales selection methods are at the root of under-performing sales teams with limited potential for growth and development.

The results of traditional sales selection systems are "below grade"

Today's CEOs and corporate leaders are not satisfied with the quality and performance levels of their sales teams, as highlighted in a recent survey by *The Harvard Business Review.* Over one hundred executives surveyed in ninety-six major corporations across seventeen industries around the world gave their sales forces an average grade of seven or about a C minus. Chances are your sales team isn't making the grade either.

Under-performing sales teams are fighting an uphill battle. First, early exits from "mis-hires" are rampant, leaving accounts and territories underserved and underdeveloped. Second, *The American Journal of Workforce Management* reports that premature turnover (exit prior to twelve months of service) costs companies anywhere from three to five times the employee's annual salary.

Do we need more reasons to challenge the status quo of traditional sales selection methods? Yes. Because this *could* happen to you:

On a cold winter's day, the national sales report landed flat on the company president's desk. The results showed that approximately 15 percent of the sales force was producing well over 65 percent of the company's sales. Why was performance so inconsistent? Meetings were held, hands were rung, and heads rolled. Sales leadership identified the issues as systemic or "organizational" and requested more marketing and advertising programs, developed more sales training events, ramped up sales support, and distributed more sales tools. These initiatives went on for nearly five years as the company doubled and redoubled its efforts to support the sales force. The result? Now the top 15 percent of the sales force was producing nearly 90 percent of the company's sales. Not exactly the outcome they were looking for—not to mention that the top line wasn't growing to match the investment. You can imagine the shape of the bottom line.

What happened? After conducting validated behavioral assessments with the sales force, the conclusion was simple and painful. Having utilized traditional sales selection processes, the company had hired some of the nicest people you'd ever want to meet—and they certainly appeared to be high potential sales associates. These were individuals who welcomed company initiatives like online learning and technical factory training; their product knowledge was a thing of beauty (i.e., they had good experience). They applauded the company's introduction of new products, they always submitted their call reports on time, and their compliance with policies and procedures was impeccable (i.e., they had good work history). They were enthusiastic at trade shows and could always deliver a customer to a company event, and their "relationships" were impressive (i.e., they had skills). There was just one big problem: they weren't wired to sell and they represented nearly 85 percent of the sales force. No, it wasn't just that they didn't know how to "close." Five years of sales training proved that. It simply wasn't in their behavioral profile to do the things top performing sales professionals do. It wasn't in their motivational profile to pursue the types of relationships and rewards that net both profitable business and satisfied customers.

On the flip side, the top performers in this group matched a benchmark profile of some of the best salespeople in this particular industry. They had the competency and the profile of true sales professionals who love the art (and science) of selling. Yet, this group complained about attending more sales training, they criticized the company's poor level of sales support, and they were frustrated by increased requirements for reports. At a critical point in the life cycle of the company, this group was ready to jump ship. Why? Because the company's sales infrastructure was unintentionally designed for people who didn't sell. Top performers are discretionary. They wanted no part of any "sales activity" they couldn't translate into a sale. They carefully calculated diminishing return and highly valued their own time. They were not interested in "reviewing" features and benefits—they lived them every day in the context of the sale.

So now what? For this company, radical steps had to be taken and the sales organization was turned on its side. Significant efforts are now underway to rebuild and refocus the sales force to attract, retain, and develop individuals who have the sales competency, the "intuitive sales fit," and the behavioral profile to sell successfully within their industry. Strategic and differentiated sales support is being targeted for top performers, and reporting requirements have been minimized and streamlined to reduce non-value activities in the field. Development opportunities are now designed for true sales professionals rather than sales stragglers who will embrace the activity but never put it into action. The company is successfully re-engaging its top performers—and is committed to a new sales selection process that balances objective and subjective inputs with a "trust but verify" approach.

Trust but verify

The PDI Sales Selection Model takes a "trust but verify" approach to the sales selection process. While it advocates throwing out the traditional *dependence* on the resume, it recognizes its basic value (along with screening interviews and reference checks) in identifying *a candidate's view and interpretation* of his or her experience, background, and work history. But before we get too bent out of shape that the resume requires more respect, let's recognize why "trust but verify" is appropriate.

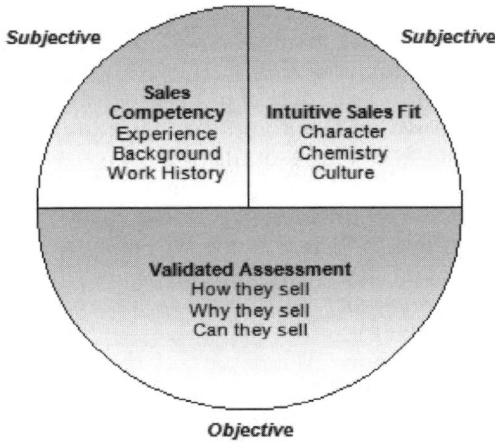

PDI Sales Selection Model
© 2007 Perpetual Development, Inc.

The proliferation of online services for resume writing and development is at an all-time high. From free resume templates (many segmented by specific role type) and position-specific content, to twenty-four hour turnaround, $9.99 "professional writing services," anyone anywhere can produce a well-crafted, "proven" resume with limited effort. Is that good or bad? It doesn't really matter. What sales executives need to understand is that today's resume isn't what it used to be. Most likely it has been designed, written, and packaged by a third party who knows how to turn a six-month stint as a clerk in a shoe store into an all-star achievement "in the competitive footwear industry." Does it mean candidates are out to deceive you? Most likely not, yet just often enough, you'd better believe it.

But who could have believed that in one of the highest profile positions in college sports one could have gotten away with falsifying information on a resume? Remember when George O'Leary resigned as Notre Dame's football coach five days after being hired? Talk about premature turnover. The cost of that exit was astronomical. Why the sudden departure? He lied on his resume. Thirty years prior, his resume claimed he had a master's degree and he didn't. He said he lettered in college football and he didn't. The inaccuracies were repeated in future resumes and biographical information, and at the age of fifty-five it was simply too late, too inconvenient, and too embarrassing to correct.

You think you can catch an inaccuracy in a resume? In hiring one of the most prominent positions in all of college sports, Notre Dame didn't—not until it was too late and far too expensive.

But there's more to consider about today's resume reviews. Advocates of traditional selection processes say that resumes can offer deep insight into the makeup of a candidate. In fact, after hearing my perspective on this topic, an individual entrenched in the HR field sent me the following e-mail:

"What is one of the most important qualities that an employer is looking for? Answer: commitment or call it loyalty or the ability to work through hard issues. The resume will show you that record and will demonstrate whether the candidate is capable of making *compounded good judgments.* And that is what really leads to success in sales or in any walk of life."

I couldn't disagree more. What part of the resume demonstrates compounded good judgments? How is commitment or loyalty measured?

Let's try an experiment. Take a look at a resume of a sales candidate who has worked for three different companies and held five different sales positions in the last fifteen years. Is the individual aggressive, upwardly mobile, and a high achiever or is he unsettled, disloyal, and an opportunist? What about the individual who has worked for the same company for twenty years and held three different positions? Is the individual steady, loyal, and a solid performer or an average performer with limited motivation and a fear of change? You may have an opinion and an educated one at that; but it is clearly subjective. And there's no question that someone else could credibly come to a different conclusion.

Interviews focused on sales competency issues are clearly helpful in identifying depth of experience, background, and work history. And most corporations have worked diligently for years to significantly improve the quality and compliance of these interviews to gather meaningful information that protects the candidate and enlightens the company. But let's face it, many of us have found ourselves in situations where we needed to place a sales associate fast. That's when we are suddenly afflicted with "behavioral blindness." We see the candidate for what we want him or her to be, not what the person really is. We force-fit the candidate into a sales position because "someone is better than no one." We convince ourselves that "sales training" will solve the inadequacies that we recognize (but we choose not to share our concerns when recommending the new person for hire).

Replace behavioral blindness with behavioral assessment

The cure for behavioral blindness is the strategic use of validated behavioral assessments designed for and tested within the sales community. Most professionals know there are a number of common personality and skill assessments that can offer general guidance for hiring and career development. Some companies have even ventured into producing their own assessments (a courageous decision in light of today's regulatory and litigious environment).

But today's better sales selection model includes specific, validated sales assessments that can *objectively* tell you whether or not candidates can sell (sales ability), how they sell (sales behaviors), and *why* they sell (sales motivators). When you integrate behavioral assessments into your sales selection process, start by identifying a trusted professional who is qualified to administer the assessment and analyze the assessment results. Then, with expert advice, identify the specific EEOC-compliant instruments you will utilize based on your industry and type of selling environment. The reports you receive should be specific to the individual and not simply offer "categorical" information for "types" of candidates.

The most valuable behavioral assessments can help identify an individual's selling style and highlight differences between an individual's "natural" and "adapted" style. This helps you get to those "born-in" or "hot-wired" behaviors while seeing what corrections or adaptations an individual is making in order to be successful under certain selling conditions. Assessments can also pinpoint the types of services and products an individual prefers to sell, how he or she handles sales presentations, and how well the individual closes and services accounts.

Let's look at a real-world example of an organization utilizing validated behavioral assessments to improve their sales selection process:

Problem: A homebuilding firm facing dramatic increases in sales rep turnover was experiencing an alarming decrease in sales. The company was fighting for survival and needed help fast.

Process: Expert analysis was utilized to evaluate the requirements for success in each sales position. A benchmark profile was established for each sales position. A selection process was identified, including both subjective and objective inputs. Validated sales assessments and targeted interview questions were implemented.

Candidate assessments and interview results were compared against the benchmark profile to establish predictors for success. Only the best candidates with the highest predictors for success were hired.

Proof: In under a year, turnover was reduced by 75 percent and sales increased by 50 percent.

By "pooling" the objective and subjective data, the company was able to take a "trust but verify" or balanced approach in the selection process. Sales management could remove behavioral blinders and see the candidates for who they really were as sales professionals. With the results of behavioral assessments in hand, both the candidates and the company had higher quality interview conversations, giving everyone the opportunity to discuss and evaluate how well the best candidates would "fit" within the organization.

Sizing up intuitive sales fit

The results of an effective behavioral assessment can also serve to objectively verify the subjective inputs used to judge a sales candidate's "fit" with your sales organization. Intuitive sales fit involves evaluating the match between your company's culture, chemistry, and character ("the three Cs") to those of the candidates'. As you size up your best candidates, and they size up your company, both parties are attempting to predict how good the match will be. Consider this scenario on culture:

You identify an excellent sales candidate with experience in the Fortune 100. The candidate appears to have strong sales competency and you are attempting to evaluate how well the individual will fit into your middle-market, privately held firm operating in a traditional industry. You suspect he is used to a far more formal and structured sales environment. He assures you he's looking for a more "relational, family-oriented team." You are concerned he may have grown too dependent upon the advanced technologies used to support his previous sales efforts. He is convincing when he shares how those tools de-personalized the sales process, something he will not compromise. He is good-looking and makes a great first impression. He has clearly done his homework, knows the product line, and would bring in a fresh perspective to the organization. Do you hire?

Let's start here: What objective data do you have to verify his (or your) prediction of "fit"? An effective behavioral assessment can show you how difficult (or easy) it will be for him to adapt his natural style to a style that matches your culture. For example, what if you learned that this individual highly values "process and procedure," "hierarchy," and "details"? By comparing his natural to his adapted behavioral style, you *and he* could see that he will experience tremendous difficulty (no matter how much he *wants* to be successful) in adapting to a new "relaxed" sales culture. Can you imagine the higher quality conversation you could now have with this candidate concerning "fit"?

What about chemistry? Certainly, you can make a subjective evaluation of a person's likeability. In his best-selling book, *Blink,* Malcolm Gladwell says that it takes two seconds to determine if you will like someone once you meet him or her. Put simply, we call this the "gut feel" when hiring salespeople. You can also make judgments about how well your sales candidate will be accepted by your customer base. There's no question that exploring chemistry on a subjective level has value. A number of sales teams excel at evaluating chemistry by placing candidates in both work and non-work situations. Whether it's a golf game (where someone's likeability *and* integrity can really be evaluated!) or a chance to walk the plant floor, you can get important insight into a sales candidate's potential for "fit."

Now, trust your gut, but verify it with the use of a validated behavioral assessment. Within the Sales Strategy Index, for example, there is a "first impression quotient" that helps to quantify the sales candidate's ability to make and hold a good first impression. It offers you a validated look at the candidate's natural and adapted behavior to see how much of a "stretch" it is to meet new people and appropriately develop new relationships. The pooling of objective and subjective data will help you and your candidate make a better determination of how well the chemistry works between the individual and your company.

Now—what about character? Frankly, I believe there's no better way to evaluate a "match" in character than to place the sales candidate in situations where the character of the company was critical to a decision or a chosen direction. While you'll want to "change the names to protect the innocent," you can re-use these "gut-check" moments to evaluate the character of your candidate. You can implement this as a written assignment or include situational questions in your interview process. The point is: don't absorb a *general* impression of your sales candidate's character. Set aside specific questions/situations where the candidate's response can reveal either a match or mismatch to the company's character.

By combining objective and subjective inputs, sales executives have the greatest opportunity for success in the sales selection process. Particularly as it relates to evaluating intuitive sales fit, this balance is critical because rarely do candidates know themselves well enough (or frankly are they honest enough) to raise the tough issues involved when matching a candidate and a company's culture, chemistry, and character.

In fact, honesty is so rare that when it happens, it's the opposite of what we expect!

The opposite of every other candidate

In the history of television sitcoms, there was never a job candidate like *Seinfeld's* George Castanza. In his bid for a key position with the New York Yankees, he decides to do the "opposite" of his natural instincts. (Translation: he decides to be honest in a job interview.)

"Tell me about some of your previous work experience," the interviewer asks.

"My last job was in publishing. I got fired for having sex in my office with the cleaning woman," Castanza accurately reports.

Stunned, the interviewer responds, "Okay, continue . . ."

"Before that, I was in real estate. I *quit* because my boss wouldn't let me use his 'private bathroom.'" Another truthful but blunt admission.

In awe, the interviewer tells George he is the complete opposite of every applicant they've seen. The interview concludes with Castanza insulting George Steinbrenner for his poor decision-making and massive ego, which is followed by Steinbrenner shouting, "Hire this man!"

Why did this comedy sketch hit a home run with the *Seinfeld* audience? Because we all know job candidates will never intentionally expose questionable character traits in an interview. It was the opposite of what we expected.

Consider "the opposite" model in sales selection

Are you relying too heavily on traditional subjective inputs to your sales selection process? Is the resume and accompanying interview the central part of your screening and decision-making? Are you predicting the candidate's "fit" with your organization based on everyone's desire and promises to make it work? If so, you might want to consider doing "the opposite."

Instead of over-prioritizing subjective inputs, do the opposite. Prioritize objective inputs such as validated behavioral assessments and get to the bottom of how and why your candidate sells the way he or she sells. It's okay to trust your subjective data, but use multiple methods to verify that trust. The more effective sales selection models require at least 50 percent of the decision-making process to be reliant upon objective data. By pooling, or "balancing" your inputs, you will significantly increase the quality of interview conversation and increase the depth of analysis when determining "fit."

If you're like the over one hundred surveyed CEOs representing ninety-six corporations in seventeen different industries, your sales team has room for improvement. What are you doing about it? I've seen many companies attempt to raise sales performance by implementing new training programs. I'm an advocate of continuous learning, but the approach could easily be off the mark. I've seen others work to inspire new sales through incentives and reward systems. This is a great way to encourage top performers, but it will do nothing for your bottom feeders. They're likely not motivated by money to begin with.

If your sales selection process offers you depth of insight into the behaviors and motivations of your sales candidates, then you will not only use that to identify the highest potential candidates, but you will continue to use that objective data to effectively retain and develop your team. Revisiting the behavioral assessments at key points in the development process will also increase the quality and outcomes of performance reviews and advancement plans.

Throw out resume "dependency"

Throw out the resume? Okay, not completely. But it's time to throw away the traditional over-dependency placed on the subjective inputs to the sales selection process. Traditional subjective selection systems are at the root of underperforming sales teams. The evidence appears in the form of high turnover, higher costs, and in some cases, embarrassing mis-hires that are motivated by behavioral blindness, too much trust, and not enough verification. With the right expertise and an effective sales selection model, you *can* recruit, hire, retain, and develop a top performing sales team that fits the chemistry, culture, and character of your company.

Meet Brent Patmos...

BRENT PATMOS is President and CEO of Perpetual Development, Inc. He is an accomplished author with published works including *Speaking of Success*, Driven *to Sell™, Success Talk™,* and *Focus on Results™*. Brent also holds the highest levels of certification as a Professional Behavioral and Values Analyst. His sales development success and quantifiable results have made him a sought-after consultant, speaker, and trainer. As a result, *Selling Power* magazine lists Perpetual Development among the top sales consulting companies in the United States. Brent is a member of Rotary, a professional member of the National Speakers Association, and holds numerous awards and recognitions for his achievements.

Brent Patmos, CPBA, CPVA
President & CEO
Perpetual Development, Inc.
Phone: 480.812.2200
www.perpetualdevelopment.com

7
James Carter

Make Business Personal

What is the silver bullet I have seen over and over again in great organizations? It's the people. People make the difference in good and great organizations.

This is nothing new. We have been told this for years.

In my experience, the more emotionally involved people are, the more effective they are. And if the difference in great organizations is its people, connect them emotionally to what they do.

But how is it done?

Years ago I learned the most valuable business tool I have ever witnessed through a company in 2000.

The best thirty minutes that this company spent with new employees, regardless of position, was to sit down with them individually during orientation and show them exactly how they made money for the company.

Armed with this knowledge, each employee knew how they contributed to the bottom line and the value they brought to the organization. It did not matter what the position was – customer service, clerical, warehouse, etc. – that person learned the value they brought to work every day.

While I was working with a particular company's training and development department, there was a new training coordinator who was hired. She was responsible for the training of all the new college graduates coming in during their initial thirty-day training. She made arrangements for them to live, eat, train, and she planned and coordinated every aspect of their life.

She was frustrated from almost the first day. The new-hires were young, cocky, and were hired at three times, or more, the salary this training coordinator was making.

Because the company was busy, it was three weeks before her boss sat down with her and showed her how she made the company money. She only made the company a small amount of money each day—around $35 per day.

Almost overnight her attitude changed. She became focused and driven.

One day, someone in the department was printing out materials and overnighting them to New York. The New York office had a printer that was connected to the company's server. All that was needed was to have the materials print at the New York office. But someone in New York did not want to put everything into binders so the request was made for someone at the San Francisco office to bind it and ship it overnight.

The training coordinator found out and had what I now think of as a textbook "conniption fit." It was the first time I had seen something like that.

The overnight package was going to cost almost $100 which meant she would have to work for three days just to make up the difference for shipping.

The person doing the printing? Her boss.

What would you do? I would probably just let it go. It is the boss!

Not this training coordinator. She stopped what was happening and when the boss confronted her, she pointed out how much money it was costing the company and how the boss was devaluing her work.

While this is one story, the company was filled with people just like this—heroes who were driven to increase the bottom line of the company.

Another company in the mental healthcare industry was having a difficult time with staff turnover and the lack of compassion in staff.

To better help their staff better understand their patients, they were given special headsets to wear during a few shifts.

While working their shift, they would hear random noises and voices through the headset. It was extremely distracting and the staff complained at how difficult it was to work while that was happening. Many were found taking the headsets off during work.

After it was framed to them as an opportunity for experiential learning, they were broken into groups to talk about what happened, why it was so difficult and how they could better help the patients.

In this case, the staff understood what an effect of calm, reassurance and compassion they have on some of these patients. They recognized the value of treating the patients with dignity, and in doing so, recognized the value in their day to day job.

The program was so successful that now new employees can be seen during their first weeks wearing headsets while working. By the way, turnover is down, job satisfaction is up and laughing and smiles are more common.

People *want* to feel valuable. People *want* to feel that the work they do matters and makes a difference and they're not just marking time.

Take the time to connect your people with what truly matters.

For example, take the accounts payable department at a pharmaceutical company, on a field trip to see the patients they help.

Have your sales team visit the patients who benefit from the product they sale, and get to know them. Send your receptionist to a closing or home inspection of a first-time buyer (if in real estate.)

Each one of us has a customer that benefits from our work, or perhaps the charities we support.

With just a little concentration and focus you can personalize your business.

Make sure every employee understands the value they bring to the organization.

If you connect your employees' hearts with the work they do, you can expect higher employee retention, increased employee loyalty, higher customer satisfaction, and the list goes on.

Create your own company of heroes.

Meet James Carter...

JAMES CARTER is Founder and CEO of Repario Ltd. *Repario* is Latin, meaning "to renew or restore" and is at the heart of what drives not only James, but the heroes involved with Repario. Working with all levels of organizations and speaking at conferences, James has been connecting people back to what matters for over fifteen years.

James Carter
Repario Ltd.
Phone: 800.513.8759
www.Repario.com

8

Lea Strickland

One Great Idea: Focus for Success

What is the single most important strategy that fits every organization? *Focus!* Focus on the customer. Focus on the market. Focus on the core competencies of the organization. Focus on maximizing the return on each project and the business. Focus on acting ethically. Focus on delivering on the commitments made. Focus on deploying resources efficiently and effectively. Focus on understanding the outcomes of positive and negative results. Focus on identifying objectives, milestones, and timelines. Focus on deliverables and accountability. Focus on communication. Focus the organization toward achieving specific, measurable, objectives. Focus on the pursuit of stated objectives. Focus on identifying and selecting executable strategies that take into consideration the resources, capacity, and capability of the organization today. Focus on how to acquire resources needed to take the organization toward its long-term goals.

There is nothing that can bring an organization to the brink of failure faster than a lack of focus. A lack of focus can be a result of many things—inexperienced management, poor leadership and organizational culture, even the ego of the business or its leader(s). When an organization loses its focus, it begins to spread resources too thin among projects, to pursue too many opportunities, and to take on tasks and activities that are beyond the skills and abilities of the team. Without focus, the organization is unable to capture the full potential of any opportunity.

Conversely, an organization capable of focusing on specific objectives can generate success in the most competitive of situations and adverse conditions. Why? Because the organization takes its limited resources (every organization has limited resources, whether it is time, money, capacity, or people), and maximizes the returns it is able to generate. How does focus maximize outcomes?

First, to focus the organization requires an understanding of its existing operations and activities—what it is, what it does, and what resources it has. Second, it takes an understanding of current and past successes and failures.

Third, it takes a vision for where the organization is going. What will the organization be and do in the future? The vision will drive the objectives and goals set over future periods, as well as the actions which must occur today and in the near term to move toward that vision.

Fourth, the organization must align its actions and its intentions toward the desired vision. Alignment requires an understanding of objectives and priorities. Imagine you have three objectives and a limited number of resources. How does the organization know what to do if a conflict arises in allocating the limited resources? By executing the fifth tenant of focus—setting priorities—the business makes rules and provides guidance for making decisions and knowing "first things first."

In order for the organization to achieve full focus, it must be able to translate its priorities into responsibilities, accountabilities, and deliverables for every level and every role in the organization. This sixth tenet of focus means that everyone has clear direction on what to do and how to deploy resources.

Ultimately, focus is translated into the organization not only through stated objectives and executable strategies, but through a conscious design of the organization and its operations. The seventh tenet of focus is to create an organization which supports the objectives and enables the strategies to be executed. Creating an operational structure that is effective and efficient and gets results means that team members are selected on the basis of needed skills, abilities, and experience. The capacity of the organization is looked at in terms of where the organization's operations are limited and how the organization is constrained. The ability to generate results— revenue, profits, services, market share, cash—is a factor of how processes are working and activities are resourced.

The eighth tenet of focus is the ability of the organization to provide resources: people, equipment, and capital (money) is a result of three components. The first component is the ability of the organization to raise investment in the organization, whether that is to obtain a loan or issue debt securities or whether it is getting individuals and other organizations to invest through equity (stock). The second component is the ability to generate a return on "idle" funds—those not deployed into operational projects—through short-term and mid-term investments outside the organization. Finally, the "proof" of the organization is the ability to generate a return on resources used in the business to do business—the projects, processes, and activities that are the core activities of the *why* your organization exists. The organization that is able to generate revenues, profits, and positive cash flow from its activities is a healthy, focused organization.

The ninth tenet of focusing the business is making the connection between results and activities. Whether you hit the target or you miss, it is important that the organization invests in understanding how the result (positive or negative) was achieved. It isn't sufficient to look at a project that met objectives and say "we're good." The focused organization wants to know why it was successful, if the full measure of success was achieved, and how success was achieved.

The tenth tenet of focus comes from the need to understand the connection between actions and outcomes, projects and returns. Number ten in the focus countdown to success is being a learning organization. Learn through internal analysis and external benchmarking. Learn through acquisition of external talent and education and training of internal team members who have a history with your organization. Learn from the squeaky wheels and misfits in your organization. Learn from the success stories within your team. Don't take any success at face value—make sure it really is a success. It may be that you hit the targets; it also may be the targets were too low.

Tenet eleven is know whether the success is real or just a perception. Sometimes a project appears successful—a deal seems to be a win—when in reality, in order to achieve the project returns, some other part of the business (usually a mid-term to long-term objective) is sacrificed, abandoned, or damaged. The decisions made in order to achieve the project objectives were made to get the short-term glory or reward while knowing that for the long-term benefit of the company's overall vision, the project needed to "fail."

Tenet twelve is make sure that performance is measured in terms that take into consideration overall organizational performance (including the long term objectives), as well as individual and project measures. If short-term or solo performance determines whether or not a bonus is paid or a raise is given, then the decisions made will usually be limited to those that will ensure the reward is obtained. People are conditioned to pursue the reward. When you associate reward with behavior, expect decisions and actions to align with receiving the reward, not with those activities and actions that won't generate the reward. Don't send mixed signals by rewarding one behavior and asking for another.

The twelve tenets of focusing your business are underpinned with five functional perspectives illustrated in the acronym F.O.C.U.S.™ (a trademark of F.O.C.U.S.™ Resource, Inc.) or processes which create an integrated approach to organizational success: finance (the numbers and the results), operations (the processes and the activities), commercialization (the market and the "product"), utilization (the resources and the capability), and strategy (the means and the methods). Focusing the activities of the organization across functional perspectives enables the organization to generate a complete analysis and understanding of the trade-offs and synergies between projects and across time.

Success is measured not at a single moment in time or measure. Increased revenues as a measure of "success" aren't sufficient to understand the impact on the organization. Instead, the organization needs to know the cost of generating those revenues at the sales level (cost of sales) and an operational level (expanding the capacity and/or support structures within the organization). Another measure of success, market share, is another measure that cannot stand alone. Market share increase without maintaining profitability and positive cash flows can actually translate to a decrease in profits and in the ability to compete. Cash is needed for growth, if you sacrificed profit margins directly through price concessions or through extended credit terms then you may find that the increase in market share doesn't translate to stronger performance and results. Sacrificing profit margins decreases true profitability of a project because of the financing and carrying costs you assume instead of your customer *and* you don't have funds available for use on other projects. In this case you might find that the increase in market share doesn't translate to stronger performance and results.

Focus is a result of conscious intent. Defining the organization, its purpose, and its activities in terms that recognize the long-term vision and take into consideration the near-term realities, requires an understanding of the components of business and how to identify alternatives, analyze options, and evaluate results. It isn't sufficient to be good at sales when you have to deliver the "goods" you are selling. It isn't enough to market the business to investors, prospects, and customers if the business doesn't have the capacity and capability to deliver the returns you have promised. Sound financial strategy is meaningless without the ability to generate sales. Large market potential will not result in financial returns without the capability to capture customer base.

Success today is a matter of honing operations to achieve the necessary degree of focus to enable the business to maximize the resources available to generate financial and operational results.

Meet Lea Strickland...

LEA STRICKLAND is President/CEO of F.O.C.U.S.™ Resource, Inc. a national business consulting firm focused on strategic financial and operational issues. Headquartered in the Research Triangle Park region of North Carolina, Lea's clients include for-profit (service and manufacturing) companies, traditional and emerging/growth industries (technology, life science, bio-tech, info-tech, pharmaceutical), not-for-profit, and institutional/government organizations. Lea is a keynote speaker, columnist (over three hundred published articles), and author of *Out of the Cubicle and Into Business.* Lea's practical approach and advice garnered appearances in three issues of *Entrepreneur*™ in 2005 and 2006 addressing start-up, growth, and management topics. She currently publishes three complimentary F.O.C.U.S.™ newsletters.

Lea A. Strickland, MBA CMA CFM CBM
F.O.C.U.S. Resource, Inc.
Telephone: 919.234.3960
www.FOCUSResourcesInc.com
E-mail: Lea@FOCUSResourcesInc.com
Newsletter Subscriptions: Newsletters@FOCUSResourcesInc.com

One Great Idea

9

Richard Fenton
& Andrea Waltz

The Greatest Success Strategy in the World!

What would you think if we told you there was a success strategy so powerful it could deliver immediate results . . . so simple it can be learned in less than a day . . . and so reproducible that anyone could master it? Well, there is just such a strategy and we're going to tell you exactly what it is, in just three words. *Ready?*

Go for No!

What we're suggesting is that to be more successful—*sometimes massively more successful*—the most reliable strategy is to dramatically increase your failure rate; in other words, the number of times you hear the word, *"No."* Of course, it's more complicated than that because the trick is in *how* you do it. But, in short, if you can fail, *you can succeed!*

"No"—The Most Empowering Word in the World!

Everyone loves the sound of the word, Yes! It's so positive, so empowering. And then there's No. For most people, No is just the opposite—negative, draining, the antithesis of Yes. But what if everyone's wrong? *What if No could actually be the most empowering word in the world?* What if you could achieve every quota and hit every income goal by simply hearing No more often?

As kids we weren't fazed at all when we heard No. We shrugged it off, laughed at it, and flicked it away like a bug. But somewhere along the line our natural sense of tenacity was lost or worse, it was drummed out of us.

But what if, starting today, you could get that tenacity back? What if, starting today, the word No stopped stopping you? What if, starting today, every time you heard the word No you became stronger, more powerful, and more resilient? And what if hearing No actually started being . . . *fun!*

Well, it can. And the results are often dramatic.

This is Not a Theory

Usually, at this point, people start thinking, *"That's an interesting theory."* Well, this is no theory.

Achieving increased levels of success by intentionally increasing your failure rate is a proven fact. The concepts contained in our trademarked *Go for No!®* program have been used, field-tested, and have helped thousands of individuals and organizations achieve unheard of levels of success. Consider the following *success stories* that have come about as a result of people *making a conscious decision to increase their failure rate:*

- One client reported a *5 percent increase* in sales across an entire division *within ninety days* of completing *Go for No* training . . .
- A mall-based retailer reported a *58 percent increase in customer loyalty program sign-ups* within thirty days of making a conscious decision to increase their failure rate . . .
- A young woman new to network marketing who, after reading our book, *went on to sell the most new accounts of any rep in her company (*Go for No! *is now required reading for every new rep in the organization!)* . . .
- A major video sales and rental chain reported a 10 percent increase in sales across the entire chain (more than 2,000 stores!) . . .
- The Branch Manager at a security systems sales organization reported that his "dread of hearing the word No" vanished and that the Go for No technique was influential in helping him increase sales . . .
- The president of a large financial services organization reported that their "quoting numbers almost tripled in the sixty days" after having their people read our book . . .
- A prominent department store chain said that the associates who had been through one of our training programs sold *$40 more per hour* than associates who hadn't . . .
- A major player in the intimate apparel industry reported a $3.50 increase in their average sale and a *$500,000 increase in gross sales*. And that was *per month!*

Admittedly, the reaction to the Go for No concept is often one of skepticism. And this skepticism is fueled by the fact that we don't suggest that people learn to *overcome rejection* or *fight their way* through failure or *tolerate no* to get to *yes. We teach people to embrace failure,* to actually start *seeking* opportunities to hear No, and to eventually learn to *love it!* We actually advise that people stop setting yes goals (goals for quotas and other targets) and start setting No-Goals™—goals for the specific number of times they intend to get *rejected* by prospects!

Sound ridiculous? Well, as ridiculous as it might sound, individuals and organizations that learn to harness the *power of No* can often achieve success in proportions greater than they've ever imagined. As one insurance industry executive wrote in a letter to our office: *"The concept contradicts everything we have been taught over the years."* He then went on to say that they found: *"If an individual can incorporate the principles into their daily selling life, the results are unbelievable."*

Yes is the Destination. No is How You Get There!

Most people get to the sign marked "failure" and figure they're heading in the wrong direction. They turn around and head back home, figuring that success must be back the other way. But it's not! When you reach the sign marked "failure"—when people start telling you No—success is almost always straight ahead.

For many the very idea of failing is enough to stop them dead in their tracks, while success is an often a mythical, nearly *magical concept,* which becomes a lifetime pursuit. Who doesn't want to be seen by others as a *"success,"* not to mention all the "stuff" that comes with it? This is why so many people will do virtually anything and sacrifice so much to achieve it—anything, of course, *but fail.*

And therein lies the rub.

Because failure is simply an undeniable sign of progress toward a goal, and to be massively successful, *you must fail more.* The problem is that most people tend to think in absolutes, and in the minds of people with rigid thinking, opposites must be exactly that—*opposite.* They have difficulty allowing failure and success to coexist on the same end of the performance spectrum.

In short, the word No has gotten a dirty rap! Most people simply think of yes as good and no as bad—complete opposites of one another. But, in reality, they're not. *They are simply opposite sides of the same coin.* They're companions—one the hero, the other a sidekick. But, as in the movies, the hero gets all the glory while the sidekick is left to tend to the hero's horse.

The Problem is FEAR

While the *Go for No!* is easy to understand and can have an immediate and dramatic impact on results, there is one main obstacle that needs to be overcome and that obstacle is Fear. Specifically: fear of failure, fear of rejection, fear of looking like a "shark" trying to *push* things on people. For example, consider the results of a survey of several hundred salespeople and sales managers who visited our GoForNo.com Web site:

First we asked: What is the biggest fear on the part of a salesperson?
- 51 percent said that the customer will say "no" and reject them.
- 22 percent said upsetting the customer by coming across pushy or aggressive.
- 18 percent said *not* making the sale or reaching their sales goal.
- Only 9 percent said they were concerned that the product was right for the customer.

Next, we asked: What is the number one quality of a great salesperson?
- 38 percent said the willingness to face rejection.
- 22 percent said ability to close for the sale.
- 18 percent said communication and negotiation skills.
- Only 5 percent said product knowledge.

The impact of fear on performance cannot be ignored. And individuals and organizations that do ignore it do so at their own peril.

Your N.Q. (No-Quotient™) is more Important than Your I.Q.

As everyone knows, I.Q. stands for Intelligence Quotient. But the number that *really* matters in business and in life is your N.Q.—your No-Quotient™—the number of times you are willing to fail, to get knocked down and get back up, knowing full well that you are almost certain to get knocked back down again. *That* is the number that determines greatness in today's competitive world.

So, what's *your* failure quotient? How much failure can you endure on the road to success? How many times are you willing to hear No and keep moving forward? These are not rhetorical questions because when you look at the great successes of our time and you peel away the outer layer—the glitz and glamour of what is seen on the surface—what you discover are "successful failures" with enormously high No-Quotients™.

Indeed, maybe the time has come to give No the credit it deserves. You must get rid of the notion that your choices are success *or* failure.

For those who wish to succeed in today's world, the only real choice is success—*and* failure.

Meet Richard Fenton & Andrea Waltz...

RICHARD FENTON AND ANDREA WALTZ are founders of *Courage Crafters, Inc.,* dedicated to helping sales, marketing, network marketing, and retail organizations increase their level of success by dramatically increasing their failure rate. Authors and creators of *Go for No!®* as well as the *Building Go for No!® Courage,* and *The "Go for No!" Leader* training programs, they have delivered over 500 workshops and keynote presentations to organizations like *CompUSA, High Performers International, Automotive Fleet & Leasing Association, Discovery Channel, Ameriprise Financial, Eddie Bauer, Washington Bankers Association, Kodak, Samsonite,* and *Meeting Planners International.*

Richard Fenton and Andrea Waltz
Courage Crafters, Inc.
790 SE Fairwinds Loop
Vancouver, WA 98661
Phone: 800.290.5028
www.GoForNO.com

10

Keith Lawrence

TIME:
Transparently
Integrated
Modern
Enterprise!

Time is a commodity, as many leaders believe. Time is money as some say. Time is a critical resource we use to deal with problems and manage our business. For example, we schedule key meeting times, buy time for advertising, count time for deliverables, time payments for cash flow, and much more! However, when any organization wants to improve, the issue is how much time do we have? In other words, how far ahead is the competition—a month, a year, five years? How much time before our resources run out? How much time is left in the strategic plan to accomplish our goals? How much time do we have to gather enough resources needed to succeed, and how much training time is needed? In most organizations people center their activities on the management of time! The problem is that most of us don't treat time as a capital resource.

Time is, for all practical appearance, in abundant supply. We are rationed the same amount of hours each day. When it comes to running our businesses or organizations we think of time typically as a scheduling event. The real issue of time comes into play usually after the fact—after the fact that we have wasted much of it and now it appears in short supply. Time is a deceptive resource, here one moment and gone the next!

In science we learn that time speeds up when traveling at the speed of light. Think of a modern enterprise that same way. With the current pressures of globalization, technological advances, increased competition, and workforce diversity, time is speeding up for all of us! Ask any CEO today and he or she will tell you that we just don't seem to have as much of it as we did a few years ago. For the leader of today and tomorrow, learning how to manage using time as a resource is a necessary skill for survival and to gain competitive advantage. Getting that advantage using time requires a simple but profound new way of thinking.

Think of the word "time" as the solution within itself. The word "time" holds the key to this new thinking. I tell leaders a simple but effective way to use time as a combat multiplier or an advantage builder:

Transparently Integrated Mature Enterprise = (TIME)

I have used this line of thought over the years with great effect. The idea is centered on the pairing of the words, "transparently integrated" and "mature enterprise." You might ask what does this have to do with the concept of time for the modern organization? Here's the reality: we as leaders usually don't have enough transparency in our work. We are not as integrated with our processes and systems as we might think. Typically we still manage with what I call "old world reporting tools" even though we are operating in the connected information age. This in many ways limits our ability to get the most out of our current information systems and pegs us into the standard way of managing as we did up until the start of the current age!

The second part—mature enterprise—is just as simple to understand. The idea of a mature enterprise is one that can face its weak points with candor, openness, and limited politics, all of which can waste time and precious resources if not embraced.

The concept of time I am proposing is based on experience. All too often I have encountered organizations that can't face transparency in their management style. This will limit the effectiveness of even the most modern information systems. Ultimately this will demonstrate a kind of deficient emotional maturity across the total enterprise and lead to catastrophic waste of resources. Without a willingness to have a culture of transparency throughout the enterprise that integrates information systems, human systems, and real-time reporting, time can slip away across the organization. My point is this: people in any organization who operate under a lack of proper information and have a limited view across the enterprise along with limited access to strategies will be world-class time-wasters.

Let's break down the concept of time as proposed in this concept as follows:

Transparently. In this sense, "transparently" is the understanding that all aspects of what an organization does needs to stand in the light of day for all to see. This is the first rule for getting the most from managing in the moment or up to the minute. Acting with the intention to gain a transparent view in all that the organization does and how the organization manages will lead to improvement in time management. By demonstrating this intention, the first and most difficult hurdle has been reached. If any organization has a culture of openness, inclusion, and a respect for its people, then the other aspects of the time equation will be achievable. Having a mindset for transparency is just making the acknowledgement that all across the enterprise there are data, reports, compartmentalized areas of information, warranty, customer complaints, development, marketing information, and much more.

The point is, what are we doing with all of this? Modern organizations collect vast amounts of data but unfortunately are not always well prepared to utilize all the information! The first step is to recognize that the organization must use such data to achieve some advantage and improvement with a very transparent view.

Integrated. As a word by itself, "integrated" is not that powerful and is overused as a management term. I have heard this term used when combined with system, as in "system integration" and in many other ways. This is not the concept I am proposing. What is important to me (and I dare say to world-class organizations) is a kind of transparency integration. When these words are used together, their individual meanings change as they make a powerful combination. When combined with integrated, transparently means the combination of human information, market intelligence, operations, customer relations, and more, all under one key philosophy. Integration is done now to see or to peer across the enterprise rather than to just transact items, order, list sales, and so on. The term "Transparently Integrated" starts to mean much more! It means the powerful integration of a culture that wants just a little more—the timely access and presentation of up-to-the-minute truth with the best information and data the enterprise has available! Most importantly, access to this knowledge across a broad spectrum of the organization is what is needed the most.

For systems and processes to be transparently integrated, a new approach in how systems work and the benefit they bring must be embraced. Most so-called enterprise-wide computer systems are nothing more than a better way to keep doing what we have always done! Most current systems are good at transacting data, moving material, processing work, and dealing with standard financial data.

The weakness of these systems is in displaying the outcome and consolidating up-to-the-minute results in simple visual graphics to show progress and target achievement. What usually happens, even in the most modern of enterprise-wide systems, is that often people still need to download much of the raw information, sort, and massage it to make any real use of it. (I discuss this problem more thoroughly in my upcoming book, *Transparency Shock*.) The concept is to take all key elements of data and drive this to a summary level. Developing a summary of the main areas of data and/or information and consolidating this into visual dashboards accessible across the organization without hiding much of the information is the minimum approach.

Visually transparent and integrated information that is accessible and summarized for a wide segment of the organization is not easy to achieve; however, it will bring enormous benefit in saving time and efficiency. The fact is that people are much more effective and productive when they are informed and integrated in a transparent organization.

Mature enterprise. This is the second part of the total time process. A mature enterprise is one that is totally willing to deal with the culture of transparency throughout the organization. A mature enterprise is one where management has the emotional maturity to carry the torch for driving a culture of linked systems, processes, goals, and a wide level of access.

When I hear leaders in any organization talk about limiting access, developing need-to-know meetings, hiding plans, and goals, then I would say they are not a mature group of leaders. They are not mature enough to deal with having their ideas and plans stand in the light of day. This lack of maturity leads to end-of-the-year surprises, failed product launch, constant reaction, and fire-fighting. A mature organization can handle the bitter truth, fight to limit politics, and drive out leaders who want to hold knowledge for personal gain.

Maturing an organization will lead to better management of time by having the courage to face issues and focus precious resources on the toughest issues the organization faces. An organization that has a high level of leadership maturity has leaders who can deal with issues and are able to handle the problems, not ignore them or hide from them. Administrators in these organizations will ask tough questions and they can stand the answer.

People want to know that leaders in their company have the maturity to want to see across the total enterprise using the best information the organization has available. The information must be timely, accurate, visually simple, and packed with integrity. We all know that the first thing an alcoholic must do is to admit that he or she is an alcoholic. Without this ability to face the bitter reality no progress can be made. This is the same with any type of organization. My observation is that the most successful leaders are the ones who focus on their weaknesses and are not afraid to search for and admit the truth. Mature leaders and organizations alike need their systems, processes, and people all aligned and managing with the most current data available.

The mature organization has leaders who strive to reach out across the entire enterprise for a better understanding of the current level of achievement and how the company is doing in reaching its goals. All of this implies that goals are known, methods to track performance are in place, and performance processes are up to the minute and honest. Mature leaders don't want to wait for the end of the quarter reports to have the most current information. A mature leader wants to be plugged in to the current system, follow progress, and have meetings to solve problems.

In what I call evolving or non-mature organizations, meetings are usually set to provide updates, keep the boss informed, or give a status report. Many of these types of meetings cannot be avoided. But in very mature organizations meetings are held to solve known issues, reach agreement, or set new directions, not to receive a status report! In immature organizations, most meetings are just status update meetings compromised by highly filtered data.

If others had the view I have of TIME—Transparently Integrated Mature Enterprise—they might have prevented some of the most famous corporate meltdowns over the last decade. I also believe that those organizations that already embrace this are some of the best performing companies in the marketplace. It's no secret that those organizations that can embrace this type of thinking will be in a better position to face issues, keep morale high, and drive success across the entire company.

When you think of time, think of it as a strategy to propel your organization to new levels of capability. We don't want our people wasting time. If we want to achieve any measurable level of success we usually start by focusing our time on an issue. Time is our most abundant commodity but without a good plan we will not take advantage of what we are given each day!

Meet Keith Lawrence...

Led by Certified Master Executive Coach KEITH LAWRENCE, The Transparency Group offers customized coaching, consulting, and keynote event speaking designed to help companies and their executives achieve and sustain corporate excellence in both national and international arenas. His seminars and speeches on corporate performance and execution give modern corporations and organizations the critical information needed to create high performance teams. Lawrence is also CEO of The Performance Score.com, an online corporate value chain software company.

Lawrence draws on his vast international corporate experiences. He has held key executive positions in Canada, Germany, and Asia, started his own companies and counseled countless others, giving his audiences practical, useful information that helps them succeed in global markets and keeps them talking for days!

Lawrence's dynamic, high-energy seminars and speeches offer keen insights into the business, cultural, and future challenges and issues international executives face. He will arm your executives and managers with the tools they need to successfully manage your domestic or international operations.

These seminars and speeches are a must for organizations that conduct international business or that wish to improve their current operations:

- *Corporate and executive performance and the art of execution*
- *Global business challenges and the coming innovation age*
- *Leadership—high performance individuals and teams*
- *Management transparency for the twenty-first century*

Keith Lawrence, President
The Transparency Group
Phone: 913.486.5125
www.thetransparencygroup.com

11

Ann E. Williamson, PhD

I Think I Can, I Think I Can, I Think I Can

"When things go wrong as they sometimes will;
When the road you're trudging seems all uphill;
When the funds are low, and the debts are high
And you want to smile, but have to sigh;
When care is pressing you down a bit
Rest if you must, but do not quit.
Success is failure turned inside out;
The silver tint of the clouds of doubt;
And you can never tell how close you are
It may be near when it seems so far;
So stick to the fight when you're hardest hit;
It's when things go wrong that you must not quit."

—Unknown

"Be like the little engine that could. Keep saying to yourself, 'I think I can, I think I can, I think I can.'" Isadora would tell me (Isadora was my mom). I remember that when I was just a little girl my mother would say these words to me. Isadora was a multipreneur, a person of many businesses—an African-American woman ahead of her time. I heard these words most of my life. My mother was a woman of strength and determination. She was a woman of character who led by example. Therefore, these words, I think I can, I think I can, I think I can, were not just words but her mantra or creed that she herself lived.

As I continue to live, I see that Isadora was right. She was right to set the intention of never giving up if you keep your eyes on the outcome or as some people may say, "the prize." She kept a positive mental attitude as long as she lived. This legacy has been handed down to me. I hope that I too have given this gift to others whom I have met and will come across during my life's journey. Having this philosophy instilled in me for a lifetime, I too believed that there was nothing I could not do.

As I became an adult, I translated the phrase "I think I can" into one word: "perseverance." What is this thing called perseverance? A definition of "perseverance," taken from the Merriam-Webster Online Dictionary states that perseverance is "the action or condition or an instance of *persevering* or persisting in or remaining constant to a purpose, idea, or task in spite of obstacles."

I came to the conclusion that perseverance must be comprised of three key components. These three key components are purpose, passion, and commitment. They formed the equation, p + p + c = perseverance. Purpose, passion, and commitment—three very powerful words—are the driving force behind, in, and around this thing called perseverance.

We will look at each of these powerful words in this equation individually, and then put them all together to form the concept of perseverance.

The first variable, P, is for Purpose

"To everything there is a season, and a time to every purpose
under the heaven:
A time to be born, and a time to die;
A time to plant, and a time to pluck up that which is planted;
A time to kill, and a time to heal;
A time to break down, and a time to build up;
A time to weep, and a time to laugh;
A time to mourn, and a time to dance;
A time to throw away stones, and a time to gather stones together;
A time to embrace, and a time to refrain from embracing;
A time to get, and a time to lose;
A time to keep, and a time to throw away;
A time to tear, and a time to sew;
A time to keep silence, and a time to speak;
A time to love, and a time to hate,
A time for war, and a time for peace."
—Ecclesiastes 3:1–8

"First say to yourself what you would be; and then do what you have to do."
—Epictetus

It is stated in Wikipedia, the free Internet encyclopedia, that purpose, in its most general sense, is the anticipated aim that guides action.

According to some schools of thought, purpose is vital to living a good life. Helen Keller wrote that happiness comes from "fidelity to a worthy purpose" and Ayn Rand wrote that purpose must be one of the three ruling values of human life (the others are reason and self-esteem). Other beliefs hold that God gives purposes to people and that it is their mission to fulfill these God-given purposes. Yet others cling to the fact that purpose is not innate, but instead freely chosen by each of us.

Some people may discover that their purpose is in pursuing a career, raising a family, devotion to a cause, or helping the needy. All of these make one's life more meaningful.

I believe that my purpose in this lifetime is to be a conduit of God's love and wisdom through teaching the truth in schools, women's organizations, and for those who will hear me speak. I also believe my purpose is to spread joy and love to those who have a hard time seeing the truth for themselves. This may be demonstrated in many ways.

The question that you may be entertaining now is how do you discover your purpose in life? There are many roads to accomplish this. The more open and accepting you are to this process and the more you think it is going to work, the sooner it will work for you.

To discover your true purpose in life, you must first clear your mind of all that is not true of your being. Then follow these steps:

- Take out a blank sheet of paper or begin to keep a purpose journal.
- Write at the top on the second page, "What is my true purpose in life?"
- Get in touch with your inner self or your higher power through meditation or movement.
- Follow your heart.
- Begin healing areas in your life that have been wounded.
- Go with the flow of the Universe.
- Revisit your interests, passions, dreams, and the wishes of your childhood.
- Create a summary statement of your life and see if you can refine that into a life purpose statement.
- Define success for yourself.
- Work with a coach.

Follow these suggestions and you will find your true purpose in life. Thus, the first variable in the equation is purpose.

The second variable, P, is for Passion.

"The most powerful weapon on earth is the human soul on fire."

—Field Marshal Ferdinand Foch

"When you set yourself on fire, people love to come and see you burn."

— John Wesley

Now let us look at the word "passion." We talk about having a passion for this or a passion for that. We use this word in our everyday language. But what is passion? Passion is knowing what you want and stopping at nothing until you get it.

We can substitute "passion" with strong feelings, enthusiasm, pleasure, or even excitement. By looking at these words we can say that passion must come straight from the heart. This definition of passion is taken from the Internet.

Ask yourself this question, what is my passion? Is it playing a musical instrument or singing? Growing house plants? Knitting or crocheting Afghans? Cooking gourmet meals? Taking pictures? Writing or reading poetry? What is it that sets your soul on fire?

The burning passion within me is to sing and speak words of joy to those who are in pain and to help alleviate suffering by speaking the words of truth, love, and joy. I have a passion for growing house plants. Watching them grow gives me such joy. I love writing poetry about my life experiences. Here is an example of my passion, poetry.

This is what sets my soul on fire.

Deep in my heart
Deep in my soul
Deep in my mind
I feel it
I know it
The fire
The glow
The power
To explore
To move
To grow
Living in passion
I am alive

Passion is a present from Spirit united with the sum of all the experiences we've lived through. Passion enables us to triumph over hindrances and to see the world as a place of infinite potential. Passion has its own force that is visible and moving within the flow of Spirit. Being passionate helps us to live a fearless life. When we do this, we are more willing to take risks that come with living life to its fullest. Again, we must trust ourselves to be receptive to experiencing every second of every hour, of every day to its fullest.

Here is another question that you may be asking yourself: how do I identify my passion? The answer is: just as you discovered your purpose. Follow these simple directives to answer the above question:

- Find a quiet place so that you can become centered.
- Take this time to identify your talents, gifts, or hobbies.
- Write them down in your journal and write the answers to the following questions in your journal too:
- What is important to me in my life at this time of my life?
- Am I overlooking anything that could be an opportunity for me to explore my passion?
- Am I discounting anything in my life right now that demonstrates my true talents?
- If I were living my passion, what would I be feeling?"
- What are the things that you do that ignite the flames of passions with in your heart and soul?
- Make the shifts to these things and live your life in a way that passion is always driving or guiding your life.
- Or if you can't do it yet, act as if, or "fake it 'til you make it."

If you take the time to put these actions into practice then you may be able to rekindle the flame of passion in your life or even discover what that passion is in your life. The second variable in the equation is for passion.

The last variable is C for commitment.

I am only one, but still I am one. I cannot do everything, But still I can do something. And because I cannot do everything I will not refuse to do the something that I can do.

—Edward Everett Hale

The irony of commitment is that it's deeply liberating—in work, in play, in love. (Part of a quote from *The Way I See It #76, Starbucks Coffee.*)

—Anne Morriss

The relationship between commitment and doubt is by no means an antagonistic one. Commitment is healthiest when it is not without doubt but in spite of doubt.

— Rollo May

Commitment implies a willingness and a *sticktoitiveness*—to do something. The word "commit" comes from the Latin word *committere,* which means to connect, entrust.

When we stand behind our words, we show others our commitment. If one is committed, one's support is unbending and unending; one is eager to do anything to make the commitment happen. Commitment guides us and secures us during demanding times. Commitment exists when our actions are in total alignment with our words. When this alignment exists between the intention, our words, and putting them into action, commitment will be there and it will last long.

In other words, commitment is the glue that holds one's purpose and passion together when one is doing something new or manifesting a new idea. Remember to be committed to the process.

I have made a conscious decision to bring more joy into the world. Sometimes I may not find myself in joy. Sometimes I feel less joy. But I am committed to the process of being joy, living joy, and giving joy.

Commitment can be difficult to follow through. I have wanted to give up on many occasions; but I knew there were others depending on me. Then it becomes not about me, but more of what my purpose, my passion, and yes, my commitment, that I have silently made to myself to bring more joy into the world.

When you notice that you are wavering from your commitment or feeling that you are becoming unglued, just keep the following in mind:

- Commitment is the glue or the adhesive that keeps it altogether.
- Commitment requires becoming deeply aware of one's self.
- Commitment is making choices and not sitting on the fence.
- Commitment is reaching beyond your comfort zone.
- Commitment is having the ability to communicate with others.
- Commitment is giving up the old ways of thinking to thinking in a new way with new information.
- Commitment means having a vision that is full of greater possibilities.
- Committed individuals set goals.

Remember that commitment is as much of a process as finding your purpose and passion in life. To truly be committed, keep your eye on the final outcome or prize and it will be easier to hold it all together. The final variable in the equation is for C for commitment.

The sum total of the equation; Purpose + Passion + Commitment = Perseverance.

"Just remember, you can do anything you set your mind to, but it takes action, perseverance, and facing your fears."

—Gillian Anderson

"Perseverance is a great element of success. If you only knock long enough and loud enough at the gate, you are sure to wake up somebody."

—Henry Wadsworth Longfellow

"Fight the tendency to quit while you're behind."

—Dave Weinbaum

In life there will be setbacks or blocks that will make you change the course you started many years ago. Keeping this formula/equation in mind you will proceed to the golden pot at the end of your rainbow. A rainbow appears only when there has been rain. We have had our forty days and nights of rain. But when the rain is over the sky is clear and birds are singing their songs and the rainbow appears. The rainbow symbolizes that all is well with the universe and it is perfect the way it is.

Perseverance comes easily to those who are committed, have passion, and live on purpose. With all of the parts of the equation in place you know without a doubt that the right people will come to support you at the right time. Other skills will develop and strengthen in your life to make this journey one of ease and with grace.

There have been times when I wanted to stop and not continue on this journey. I was having what I thought were many difficult lessons to learn. The truth is that these lessons were necessary for me to fulfill my purpose in my life. I stopped—but only for a little while. I continued because I knew what my purpose was and I had a passion that was still burning in my soul. I glued it altogether with a drop of commitment. The end result was that everything turned out exactly the way it was supposed to be.

I persevered remembering the equation. I lived the words of Sir Winston Churchill: never, never, never give up! I also remembered Isadora, asking myself, what would Isadora do or say? There's an easy answer to this question. She would no doubt say, "Be like the little engine that could. Keep saying to yourself, 'I think I can, I think I can, I think I can.'"

All aboard!
I am choo-chooing
Down the track;
Going to a place I've never been before,
Never stopping,
Never stuck,
Moving right along.
I know why,
I feel it in my bones.

73

I am doing it now:
I think I can,
I know I can,
I can!
Yes, I can, can!

Meet Ann Williamson...

ANN E. WILLIAMSON is a dynamic minister, an inspirational speaker, professional coach, and educator. She is the founder of and Executive Director of a nonprofit organization called the Butterfly House, Inc. dedicated to serving women re-entering and reintegrating into society.

Dr. Williamson is the owner of Williamson Comprehensive Group. WCG specializes in coaching women who are executives, small business owners, and multi-faceted entrepreneurs.

Ann's educational background includes being a Graduate of Coach University. She has a PhD in Holistic Counseling Ministry and in Educational Administration.

She also holds a Master of Education Degree in Instructional Leadership, and in Language Arts.

Dr. Ann Williamson
Phone: 480.855.3676
E-mail: dranelwi@aol.com

One Great Idea

12

Mark J. Blackman, PhD

Survive and Grow:
The Right Support is
Vital in Business

Let's face it, starting a new business is not easy. If it was, many more would succeed than do. Sadly, the mortality rate among new and start-up businesses is quite high. True, there are those who will say that this risk can be reduced by following a proven system, such as a franchise, or by purchasing an existing business. It has been my experience that this is true, but only to a degree.

There are many franchise offerings that may enhance your survival chances considerably. However, you'll note that if you continually review listings of franchise offerings, the players change regularly. You will find that many franchisors are not able to continue support for an extended time period. Also, franchisors may offer a system that has been successful as a single operation, but insufficient attention has been given to broader operations or to mass marketing the brand. In other cases, the business model or plan may be so limiting that it is difficult for the franchisee to adapt to local market variations. Sometimes, the preparation of the new franchisee may not provide the general business background lacking in many new entrepreneurs.

Additionally, some franchisors and business offerings do not have knowledge of strict laws and regulations governing their activities in some states. In states where such laws are very strict, I'm continually struck by the ignorance of these franchisors who are not in compliance, although the penalties are quite severe. Finally, you must remember that the primary goal of a franchisor, as in any other business, is to maximize its profits; this does not necessarily mean that their system will do so for you. In either case, a perfectly successful system for one area may not work well in another; a viable plan at one time may require adjustment as social and consumer norms change.

This is true for established business operations as well. Often, as consumer trends and demographics change, the independent operator fails to remain current. This is especially so in areas of rapid population growth and business expansion. The profile of a community can be stagnant over a decade or vary markedly from one year to the next. But how do you determine all these variables? How do you even learn what information you must know to survive in the hectic world of modern business? Obviously, you can't be an expert at everything and as a prospective entrepreneur you're usually so unsure that you wonder if you know anything at all. Indeed, being unaware of how to find information you need is one of the worst places you can be in business. This can be a maximum stressor during a generally stressful time.

Well relax, there is an effective solution. I have discovered, after significant trial and error, how to determine these very important facts and obtain even more information that can be beneficial or vital to your business. In my opinion, this is a significant key to success in business. The novice entrepreneur, or one beginning an unfamiliar business venture, will soon learn that the more questions you ask, the more you'll find that you'll need to have answered. However, an important key to success is an efficient method for obtaining answers. This is true in virtually any business venture; it doesn't matter if it is a new business, a franchise, or an existing business. In fact, it's important to have this powerful tool at your disposal even if you are planning changes to, or even just operating, a successful business.

It's important that the offering, plan, or operations be reviewed by knowledgeable people who can advise you independently and do not have any other agenda other than your success, both at the outset and at regular intervals. The trick is to find this support and build a support team you can trust. There are some basic questions any businessperson must answer; at the outset, help is invaluable. For example, what necessary documents must be prepared and filed, and what information must be available? The more experienced businessperson may choose to use outside sources to help develop strategies while completing routine tasks in-house. For those with little or no experience, it's probably best to let your support team handle the entire process—at least until your understanding of it is sufficient.

The most important criterion for members of your support team is that they work for you. Although it's always wise to obtain as much information from as many sources as possible, always consider your advisors' motives and agenda. A possible conflict need not disqualify a source, but should help to evaluate its candor. Once you have established trusting relationships, leverage them fully. At the outset, you should begin by building your team with an attorney and an accountant. Rely upon their advice, especially when you lack experience in business operations. Mistakes at this time can be costly or even fatal. The old saying, "if you can't do it right, do it over," simply cannot be allowed to apply here. However, the conventional wisdom, "he who fails to plan, plans to fail," most certainly does.

Depending upon what business you are in and your level of expertise, it may be necessary to find an attorney or accountant who has expertise in your chosen field, as well as general business knowledge. Typically, these specialists may refer you to associates who offer specialized knowledge and handle your general business needs. The reverse may also be true; however, in whatever way you choose to accomplish this step, you should feel comfortable with your choices. Remember, the most solidly built structure will fail if the foundation is weak.

Frankly, you may discover that even though it may be possible for an experienced business operator to complete certain tasks, it may not be cost effective. This is a decision that must be reached by the businessperson and his or her trusted advisors. The trick is not to know the answers, but rather, what questions to ask. It's here that your support team will be invaluable. It's usually not that hard to answer many pertinent questions or perform required tasks, provided you know you need to do so in the first place. Admittedly, the wisdom in this approach is obvious, but how is it accomplished?

The key is to network and ask for recommendations for trusted experts on whose counsel you can rely. Of course, always be wary of the agendas of all concerned. Your sources and advisors will have one, everyone does, but ensure that it is transparent. If the advisor has a product or service to sell (especially if it's competing) he or she may provide general and specific information. However, you must be confident that these recommendations are unbiased and in your best interest. For entrepreneurs, it has been my experience that local providers, often verifiable and supported by local testimonials, are best at providing this quality of support. Members of neutral trade organizations, such as Chambers of Commerce, depend heavily upon their reputations and "word-of-mouth" to build their businesses. Often they operate on the premise of relationship-building rather than on the one-time sale. Advisors selected from this group generally believe it's more important to focus on community growth and mutual success than on short-term return.

In my business career, I have discovered that Chambers of Commerce offer a ready made nucleus for your individual support team. These are leads or networking groups and other similarly functioning entities. Differing from many other networking organizations, they are small groups, usually less than thirty business people. Their primary function is to meet, usually weekly, to provide business leads and other useful information. However, in the process, they can serve as a nucleus to build efficient and diverse business relationships quickly as well. In doing so, they will present your business to a wider audience; they effectively become your spokespersons. Since they usually have members who concentrate on providing business-to-business services, the members' professional contacts, which they will often share, may serve to broaden your base of advisors even further. Additionally, since they meet on more than just an "as needed" basis, they will become more familiar with your needs not only globally, but in the local market as well.

What's just as important, this personal relationship suggests to their contacts that you offer the same high quality service. This can be a powerful "word-of-mouth" advertisement that can continue virtually indefinitely. Consider the sociological concept referred to as "The Six Degrees of Separation." Basically, sociologists tell us that if you start with two people and continue to branch out to all the people they know, repeating the process six times will eventually account for the earth's entire population.

Thus, if you start with a small group where you are comfortable and can interact with all the members, say about thirty business people, the network you connect with is huge. More so, since the trust factor is transitive, you can rapidly develop and expand not only your client or customer base, but your expert team as well. It's also bidirectional, at some point you may be seen as an expert and asked to join someone else's team. Consider the networking possibilities; it ensures you will have a firm basis in business that you can adapt rapidly to new and changing conditions and situations. The group will be not only be available to answer questions reliably as part of your expert team, but can also initiate suggestions that may prove useful to your operation because they are familiar with both you and your business. The cost of membership is often quite nominal and the benefits are significant.

As an example, I will discuss a typical group I have worked with. Although it is diverse, I'll suggest ways in which its membership provides support and information. Furthermore, I have referred clients to such groups to allow them to observe the utility of this dynamic firsthand, with extremely positive feedback. Most often, these groups solicit guests and invite them to several meetings. If it is mutually determined that a productive working relationship is possible, the prospect is then invited to join.

There are usually a number of these groups available locally and I strongly suggest visiting as many of them as possible. In this way you will be assured of an optimal fit in the most productive environment. Most groups have members who offer basic business-to-business services so these contacts can be easily developed. Also, by visiting groups other than one you might choose, your business becomes known to them and their members become known to you. This further enlarges prospects for your advisory team, even though you may work with them less regularly.

Many local Chamber of Commerce rules may limit the number of such groups you can join. Of course, you can broaden this base even further by joining Chambers of Commerce other than your local one. You might consider regional organizations or those in areas where the demographic is particularly suited to your business. In this case, the limitation is usually time. It's a simple business decision to determine the optimal balance between networking and operational constraints. Also, try to remember that such networking is not a fixed parameter and will vary as your business and its customer demographics grow and change. Be sure to account for this in your business plan.

As a simple experiment, during a presentation I was giving to such a group, I queried each member present to briefly suggest ways their business or services could be supportive of a new business starting in the community. In other words, could they consider being a part of its support team and working with this business to mutually grow? I'll summarize the responses to the first question; the second was resoundingly affirmative. This *ad hoc* survey was not meant to be all encompassing or inclusive, only to suggest the diversity of talent, hence expertise that could be found quickly and effectively within the group.

We immediately realized the benefit of an attorney who was an expert in small business matters, accountants who specialized in tax preparation and planning or specialized in a wide range of business applications, and commercial insurance specialists familiar with a wide range of occupations and associated risks. However, there were others that someone might only consider retrospectively and likely after a costly learning experience. One group fell roughly into physical asset planning or support. There was a home inspector who also handled commercial properties. Consider the benefit of having this insight into a planned rental or acquisition. A commercial realtor who could offer insight into market rates for commercial space could be of invaluable aid in site selection.

Consider the benefit of a light duty contractor for reliable repairs, or a respected, trusted plumbing and heating contractor ready to support you, not only in time of dire need, but in planning as well. Other building trades such as siding, windows, and landscaping might round out the team that would be in place to support your needs. Also, remember that contractors often know reliable vendors in other trades. These few contacts could provide you with an effective compass to navigate an area where mistakes can be both damaging and costly.

A commercial cleaning service was also represented. It is very surprising how this sensitive area is neglected by many businesses. Not only is this important from a sanitary standpoint, but from a security one as well. Many times I have encountered unscrupulous persons who obtained critical information during the office cleaning process. A trustworthy vendor is critical for this function.

Combined members of the group offered an effective solution for many business advertising needs. The group's printer, Web site designer, promotional item specialist, photographer, and shopper listing service could offer a combined strategy to meet many advertising needs. The computer support specialist would prove invaluable in ensuring that related critical business functions were maintained and developed. Even the healthcare, residential realty, investment specialists, and others offered both business support and trustworthy personal support as well. There was also a respected vehicle dealer who could provide the proper equipment at a fair price. All in all, the group is a good resource to have at your fingertips when the need arises.

Consider the value of your support team on the critical day in the life of your business when you need a "go-to" person who not only won't gouge you, but will come to your aid as quickly as possible. Beyond that, remember all the contacts our members have and are willing to share; consider the size and scope of the expert support you have. What's just as important, they know you offer the same quality. Remember, if you start with a small group where you are comfortable and can interact with all the members, about thirty business people, the network you connect with is enormous, virtually global.

The benefit of this good idea is reciprocal; by supporting the members of the group you enhance your reputation in the community. All of us encounter friends, customers, or clients who have special business needs or are considering either a new business venture or expanding an existing one. Also, consider the public relations benefit of such a recommendation. Based upon your own experience, think about how much easier and effective it would be for an entrepreneur to meet with a manageable group with wide and varied expertise and how this reflects upon you and your business.

Meet Mark J. Blackman, PhD...

MARK J. BLACKMAN, PHD, received his degree from Purdue University in Chemistry. His doctoral research was in Computational and Theoretical Physical Chemistry. He has more than forty years of experience in the fields of analytical, chemical, and medical instrumentation. His most recent areas of expertise include NMR (MRI); separation science and concrete technology including surface preparation, coloring, and coatings. He has participated in the development and support of new technologies, training methods, and advanced applications of existing ones. He offers this expertise to clients who require design, service, and training support for most electronic and electro-mechanical equipment used in scientific research and production operations, technical or general presentations, and seminars. Mark also has extensive security and law enforcement experience and provides clients with insight into personal, corporate, and industrial matters and practices. He has recently been speaking to, and working with, local Chambers of Commerce, as well as other civic and community groups, to promote careers in science. In recognition of his career achievements, Mark was recently selected for lifetime listing in the prestigious *Who's Who Worldwide.* He is also available for technical and general presentations or seminars. *Special consideration is offered to educational institutions or those involved in national security or public safety.*

Mark J. Blackman, PhD
Phone: 312.505.0522 (mobile)
630.551.1266 (office)
E-mail: consulting@markjblackman-inc.com

One Great Idea

13

Kelly Jahner-Byrne

Personal Velocity: Accomplishing your Earn-deavors!

Have you wondered why some people just seem to be golden? Everything they touch turns to gold. Whatever they do works magic, while others toil and don't seem to get anywhere. Their secret to success is *Personal Velocity.* Here is the good news: personal velocity people are created, not born. People don't just wake up successful. You can create your own personal velocity (or momentum) and set yourself up to succeed.

It boils down to this: it is easier to go from forty miles per hour to sixty miles per hour than to go from zero to sixty miles per hour. Personal velocity means creating and then using momentum strategically. It means you must first be willing to start. You must take your first step, then another, and another. This creates momentum that takes on a life of its own, keeping you going so you are much more likely to accomplish your objective. Slowing down, speeding up, maintaining, stumbling, encountering bumps along the road, and pit stops to refuel are all to be expected along the road to success. Just don't stop altogether or it will be that much more difficult to get up to speed again. It's the motion that's the key—the energy that comes from velocity that will help drive you to your destination.

Creating a personal velocity environment will give you the fuel and power to accomplish your personal and professional goals. Velocity powers your ideas, and keeping up that momentum gets you to your end result. Now that you understand the core concept of personal velocity, we can discuss the basic principles that make up your personal velocity and how you can apply them to your goals. By focusing on these five basic principles, you are sure to keep your momentum going.

One thing I have learned in business is that everyone has a theory, and theories change over time. Everyone has his or her own idea about how to achieve success, but are these ideas actually working? Most people spend too much time thinking and theorizing

85

and too little time *doing*. Basic principles don't change. Principles are your operational velocity. If you work to move your business forward on solid principles that can pass the test of time, then you can bypass the latest fad in business *theory* and move toward reaching your end goal. I would like to share my basic principles that have created personal velocity in my own business—my *earn-deavors*.

Principle 1. People do business with those they know, like, and trust—develop contacts!

Relationships are built between people every day. Someone you know—someone to whom you were introduced or a person you actively sought out to meet—comprise the relationships we strive to develop. Some relationships are built slowly over time, while others quickly form hard and fast. Over the years I have found that the best business deals and positive transactions I have struck are because of common interest—otherwise known as the common ground tactic. Make it a point to find something—anything!—you have in common as a relationship launching pad.

If you find others interesting, it may be because of the interest they have taken in you. If you make it a point to show genuine interest in others, they are more likely to find you interesting in return. If you think you are not interesting, then get interesting! How do you do that? Quite frankly, just leave your home. Get involved in an activity that interests you. You will surely find others in that realm, and they then will become points of contact for the future. Make sure to actively seek out and initiate relationships, and be sure to ask for and keep contact information. Most people are willing to help those who share their interests.

Get out there, get to know people, find people you like and who will like you back because of shared interests. Once you get to know and like someone, demonstrate that genuine interest in him or her. This is the beginning of building trust. Start by being trustworthy. Trust is earned over time. We all start off with a deposit in our trust bank account with an individual. It is basic human nature to want to trust other people. We either deposit or debit our account by our words and our actions. Simple actions can add to your trust account— good manners, good use of language, personal confidence, and your demeanor are just a few.

One of your best assets is your smile when it is genuine and friendly. That in and of itself adds dramatically to your trustworthiness. Make the person you are with feel welcome to talk with you. Have a good attitude, focus on him or her with your full presence, offer praise when you notice it is deserved, and people will gravitate toward you. Then follow through with what you say you are going to do—earn trust by building trust.

Principle 2. Credibility—building respect with your contacts!

Why do people do business with you? It begins with *you*. Are you credible enough that people want to do business with you? People don't wake up with credibility; it is based on their performance over time. Time is relevant, however. You can gain a significant amount of credibility through one task well done. We all have a credibility bank account. It is an extension of our trust account. We are constantly adding to it and gaining dividends or subtracting from it and leaning toward the potential for an overdraft. If we keep subtracting from our credibility bank account, it becomes increasingly challenging to gain that trust back. Always be depositing, even if just in pennies. Your credibility in business will far exceed your business bank account in the beginning, but it will take your business further in real dollars and cents later on.

There are many ways to earn credibility. *Do what you say you are going to do.* Always under-promise and over-deliver. Respect people by being on time. Say please and thank you—good manners never go out of style. These are some of the reasons people know, like, and trust you. People you meet may not need your product or service immediately, but keep in touch with them, be credible, and when the timing is right for them, you will be the source they go back to as long as you have remained easy to find. Be easy on the ears by being friendly, keeping in regular contact, and telling people that if they are in need, you want to be the one they go to. Over time this kind of transaction will pay you high dividends. The principle applied properly will allow your personal velocity to continue to grow.

Credibility is won or lost in the company you keep. People judge you and your credibility based on the people and businesses you align yourself with. Be careful to safeguard your reputation—you only have one to work with. A good reputation is gold; a bad reputation puts you out of business.

Principle 3. Business happens with posture—building confidence!

Business posture is accumulated over time, but you can accelerate your posture by taking action. Business posture—or confidence—can accumulate quickly based on actions. An individual's actions speak much louder than the volume of their words. We have all been around big talkers, but it is often the quiet doers who earn our business. Confidence and posture are accumulated business skills that can create continued personal velocity in your business because people are attracted to people who are confident. People want to be assured; they inherently shy away from risk, and they will seek you out if you have posture they think and feel they can rely upon.

Confidence is gained through experience; but how does one start out confident? Draw from your past. Everyone has had success in something in life. It could be securing that first job, scoring high marks on a test, winning a game, or even completing a hard workout. The confident feeling you had can be brought back from memory to power you forward. Everyone starts somewhere. Those with personal velocity move from simple successes to more complex successes. We have all heard that success breeds success and failure breeds failure. Be careful not to falter when you have a failure. It is the lesson learned and the confidence you gain to try again more intelligently that will power you forward to your next success.

Confidence is something I personally have worked on my entire life. I did not grow up as the best player on the field, the most popular in the class, the most intelligent, or the most skilled in the job. But I did have many small successes along the way that I drew upon and used as affirmations in my own mind so I could garner the confidence to push forward.

Anyone can do this; however, you must actually do it again and again to grow this inner confidence. It is a solid principle that you build upon. You learn by positive actions just as easily as you learn from negative actions. If you are dwelling on negative actions, then realize it and correct your course. A great way to start is to believe in yourself. Belief is defined as having confidence in the truth or value of something. Believe in yourself because you are the one person you can truly rely upon. I have found that in order to believe in yourself, you must first acknowledge that you can actually be what you believe you can be. Self-talk is a quick way to get a positive message into your mind.

When you have a shortcoming, acknowledge it, make a mental note of it, and then draw from your positive past and push forward. The quickest way to gain confidence and posture is to take action. By taking action, you will either succeed or fail. Either way, you end up more educated and insightful—you know more about what works and what does not work, and that will add to your confidence and posture.

Principle 4. Take action—doing what it takes!

Leaders with personal velocity do not confuse activity with accomplishment. How many times have you spent too much time getting ready to take action? I have spent far too much time clearing my schedule just so I could fill it again. If we spend too much time waiting for the perfect moment to take action, we will never have the time for it. We've all heard the old line, "I'll get to that tomorrow when I have more time." In reality we all have the same twenty-four hours each day to move our business and our life forward. There really is no time like the present.

We can take small steps forward that will get the ball rolling, which creates momentum. Momentum builds with each step, and before you know it, the personal velocity you've created will take hold and propel your actions into accomplishment. Take the no excuses exit, get off blaming boulevard, go straight down start street, and end up on accomplishment avenue.

Most people never get to the point of taking action because fear of failure holds them back. The reality is that everyone has fear because nobody wants to fail. However, if you don't take the first step, you get nothing. That first step is the hardest. Take a step, no matter how big or small. By the third step, you will have gained momentum. People who don't take those first few steps stay where they are because the pain of change seems greater than the pain of staying the same. Unfortunately the pain of staying the same just gets more and more intense. There is negative momentum in staying the same. It steals greatness, keeping people from reaching their true potential.

No one will hand us a great life, a great business, or great relationships. It is what you do with what you have or what you do to overcome what you lack that moves you forward. Take action. Tell yourself that if I do this one thing today, it will get me one step closer to my goal. Set your goal; make it specific. Know what your why is—the desire must come from within. It can't be taught. It has to be greater and deeper than just money. It is what makes you get up in the morning. As you take action, steep yourself in positive self-talk, and just get going. Take enough steps that you build momentum and get personal velocity rolling to help propel you forward.

Principle 5. Stay the course—achieving your goals!

Staying the course requires an inner commitment to reaching your goal long after the initial excitement wears off. As you take action, notice and celebrate all your successes—even the small ones—along the way. This will re-energize you and help you stay the course even when things get rough. Staying the course is an exercise in persistence, commitment, trust, posture, and credibility. The longer you stay the course, the more confidence you will gain. Staying the course builds on the personal velocity you have set in motion. People will see you as dependable and will want to do more business with you.

If you get off track, just get right back on course. It would be easier in the short-term to stay off course if you fall off, but it wears your confidence down and damages your credibility. So correct your course and move on. It's like being on a diet. The first few days you take action may be hard or may feel easy, but inevitably we are tempted to fall off the diet as the novelty wears off and temptations appear. Don't punish yourself unduly and wallow in self pity; just move on and get back on track. Stay confident and let your personal velocity move you toward your goal.

Most people quit just moments before they would have achieved success. It is vital to keep your goals in mind and keep moving forward. However, this principle should never be confused with going down on a sinking ship. Common sense and practical business sense should apply both in your personal life and your professional life. You wouldn't keep throwing money into a business that truly did not have the forecast and potential to succeed. Many people let their ego get in the way of what is best and don't know when to get off the course completely. They get so focused on the end result that they begin to lack good judgment.

Leaders with personal velocity tend to put measures in place to be their checks-and-balances system. This allows them to bounce ideas off their mentors and stay on course but avoid obvious pitfalls. You must know that there will be failures along the way and you'll need to make sacrifices. Be cautious because all too often an individual gets involved in a business plan or opportunity that was destined from the beginning to fail. This is when your contact list will serve you well. Advice from associates or trusted business friends who have your best interest in mind will be invaluable as you continue on your course.

Putting it all together—creating your personal velocity!

Each of the five principles is intermixed. All relate to and build off one another. If you leave out one, the result is changed. If you bake a cake and leave out an ingredient such as eggs, the result will be different. You don't have to implement the principles in a particular order, but it doesn't work well to apply one in your life and not another, as all five do interrelate.

People who successfully implement personal velocity in their lives and who inspire others to do the same realize that limiting themselves to a manageable handful of ideas and principles will keep their plan or activity in action. Leave one hand empty so it can still juggle and maneuver. If a ball drops as you juggle, just pick it back up and start juggling again. It is when you hold too many balls that you are less likely to succeed. Focus on a few solid principles and a few manageable ideas, build trusting relationships, enhance your credibility and posture, take action, and stay the course because personal velocity gets your momentum going.

In business, leaders exercise a few solid principles that stay constant. That is what gets us to where we need to go. This is our operational system—we can change or upgrade our software, ideas, theories, goals, and plans, but the principles that guide how we operate remain the same. These five guiding principles are like a rock, an anchor, a foundation—when you add them together, you can lean on them and be assured of their solidity. They keep you grounded.

As you take on your *earn-deavors* in life, put these five principles into action: people work with those they know, like, and trust; credibility is key; posture is everything; take action or else; and stay the course. If you commit to these principles daily, you will build your own personal velocity and gain the momentum that will drive you to succeed. Go to it!

Meet Kelly Jahner-Byrne...

KELLY JAHNER-BYRNE'S unique experiences and no-nonsense approach to business solutions makes her one of the most sought-after business professionals nationally.

She is an Author, Speaker, Entrepreneur, Talk Show Host, President, CEO, Board of Directors Chairwoman, Political Consultant, and she was Mrs. Minnesota 2001. She is the CEO of Kelly Enterprises, L.T.D., a firm committed to developing cutting-edge individuals and businesses. Her ability to captivate audiences through her entertaining style makes her unique.

She uses her talents and background as an award-winning talk show host and professional vocalist to train, educate, facilitate, and bring the High Velocity process to your project.

Kelly is the author of *Volunteer for Life, Achieving Your Personal and Professional Goals,* and has been featured in *Average Girl, Minnesota Monthly, TRAVELHOST, iAM* magazine, and many other publications. She has chaired a number of successful fundraising events in the nonprofit sector and is President of the Cancer Benefit Fund, a 501(c)(3) organization.

Kelly Jahner-Byrne
Kelly Enterprises, L.T.D.
Leadership, Training, Development
Phone: 651.283.8333 Direct
E-mail: kelly@kellyenterprisesltd.com
www.kellyenterprisesltd.com

14

Training You Can Grasp

It's been said today's generation doesn't want to know information—they want to know where to find it. They don't need to know how to spell (the spell check on their computer does it for them) or memorize phone numbers (hundreds are stored in their cell phones). Today's generation learns far differently than past generations. Gone are chalkboards and overhead projectors that are replaced by white boards, Webinars, and podcasts.

Research project due? No longer do you head to the library to pore through volumes of encyclopedias and reference books. Now you simply do an online search and have access to thousands of documents at the click of the wheel. Today's learners are definitely different. Heck, they think George Foreman is the "grill guy" and Paul Newman sells salad dressings for a living. They learned in a vastly different style than the previous generation of learners who are currently designing the programs for the new employees—a recipe for waste and inefficiency.

Many companies have struggled to meet the challenge of this generation entering the workforce. Boring, out-dated print materials or corny VHS-tapes (what are those?) welcome and "train" the new employee. This generation has been raised by a barrage of images from television, the Internet, video games, cell phones, text messaging, MP3 players, online chats, caller ID, and so on. Ever watch a teenager? They will have CNN on (with its scrolling stock ticker, weather, sports scores, upcoming stories, and an actual reporter on camera), be on their cell phone talking to someone while they have an online chat with five other friends—and still say they are bored! They come to work for us and we show them a manual and a video—it's an immediate disconnect.

While DVD and e-learning have provided a better method to train people, it's still not where it needs to be, partly because those creating the training (i.e., the Baby Boomers and Generation X) learned much

93

differently and don't quite understand how this generation was "coded" to obtain and process information.

Today's employee wants information in chunks—just what is needed right now right here and nothing else—it is called the p.o.d. Training™ approach to learning. The p.o.d. Training approach designs training programs in small bits grouped together by commonality (e.g., a particular job to learn). Employees scroll through the lists and find the information they need and watch or listen to it right at their work station. Once they see what to do, hands-on skill practice or role-play allows them to build the foundation one component at a time and ensures effective, quick transfer of knowledge and skill— instant skill-building and an ability to be productive quickly.

These employees want to learn what is needed, where it's needed, when it's needed—it's how they live their life so why should training be any different? Today's generation wants to control the learning experience and not be put through a training "program." These employees have had the remote in their hand since before they could walk and taking this approach to training fits right in. This group learns information in small bits or chunks and applies it versus watching long, boring video clips not relevant to what they need now or reading pages of text. These approaches are not in the mental shelf space of how they learn. For example, going on a trip and need directions? Today's generation doesn't pull out a map, it's too hard to fold back up! Instead, they get the directions online ahead of time or have a GPS system in their car.

Putting training on mobile devices—p.o.d. Training—allows the learner to be in control while providing the company not only a viable means to get into this generation's mental shelf space, but to also provide an inexpensive way to keep materials and information updated frequently.

In the past, videos and manuals were updated infrequently due to the cost of updates. New information took days or weeks to reach every employee. These employees normally don't even read the daily newspaper because it is "old news." Are those companies on the same wavelength with their employees? Do those employees say what a great place this company is to work?

By creating information in small chunks and "pod casting" it out to employees through a variety of means, companies keep all the employees (and the materials) updated and fresh. Replacing only what is obsolete or out-dated allows companies to keep costs of distribution down (no more bulky mailings of manuals or videos) and the materials are up-to-the-minute. It fits right into today's learning style of "just give me what I want when I want it."

Imagine if when each time employees plug their device into their PC, the most recent training changes are made or updated. Cell phones, PDAs, and mobile devices already do that for our contacts, calendars, and so on—the employees expect that of their training device. Instead of having new employees learn how to navigate through proprietary software on a PC, companies can provide a mobile device they already know how to use . . . and provide multiple-language formats so the employee can learn in the language he or she is most comfortable.

The innovation of p.o.d. Training isn't so much a technological solution as it is a process to address how people learn. Too often companies spend tons of money on materials for training new employees, never realizing once training is over that the training manuals or videos are never utilized again.

The new approach is not only ideal to train new employees as they go through all the components of their new job in small chunks, it also provides an outstanding video and/or audio reference tool they can have in the palm of their hand or clipped to their belt. Forget something? Navigate through with the click of a wheel or a few keystrokes and you have the information. Unsure of how to do something you may have never been shown? Click down through the menu and there is your answer!

Does it work? The only restaurant chain to ever win the Malcolm Baldrige Quality Service Award for business excellence—Pal's Sudden Service in Kingsport, Tennessee—implemented this approach and shaved 15 percent off their training time. The drive-through-only restaurants can process two hundred cars per hour during peak periods and make less than one mistake per 3,600 orders.

Speed and accuracy are essential and new employees must be brought up to speed quickly or the employee and the customer both suffer. By using the p.o.d. Training approach, employees learn one thing or one item at a time and become proficient in it very quickly. They can then learn the next skill, ensuring employee and customer satisfaction—the reason most companies are in business.

The innovation of p.o.d. Training is an ideal solution for companies with multiple locations or workforces who are geographically dispersed and addresses the needs and styles of today's generation of employees. Need to learn a new language? Learn five words at a time, practice them, and move on to the next clip. New product launch? Instantly see what it is/does and how it relates to your job and get back to the task at hand or go implement the new product. Going to the hospital? Soon your doctor may provide you with a mobile device that has reference information for you to look at while he or she is attending to other patients or for you to take home to refer to when doing physical therapy to ensure it is done the proper way.

Gone are the bulky, outdated manuals, overhead projectors, classroom-led instructors with gobs of text on presentation slides,

VHS, DVD, and so on. Instead, today's new employees receive a device they already know how to use placed in the palm of their hands to help train them on a continuous basis—p.o.d. Training. Since our "hard drives" (our brains) archive and store information in places sometimes hard to find (don't you wish we could "defrag" our brain?), processes and devices such as p.o.d. Training allow us to quickly access the information we need and move on with our lives.

Meet TJ Schier...

TJ SCHIER is the President and Founder of Incentivize Solutions and p.o.d. Training. He provides keynote addresses, consulting, and training on motivating and training today's generation to enhance service and sales. As the author of three books and over one hundred articles on customer service and training today's generation, he has been featured in *Business Week, Incentive Magazine,* and numerous trade publications. He is a member of the National Speakers Association, he is on the HR Advisory Council of the National Restaurant Association's Educational Foundation, and is a past President of CHART (Council of Hotel and Restaurant Trainers). He works with many of today's leading companies and presents dozens of times each year across North America. He has an MBA and BBA in Finance from the University of Texas and resides in the Dallas/Ft. Worth area with his family.

TJ Schier
PO Box 271170
Flower Mound TX 75027
Phone: 972.691.7378
Fax: 972.691.7578
E-mail: tj@podtraining.us
www.podtraining.us
www.incentivizesolutions.com

One Great Idea

15

Pamela Robinson

Great Leaders Build Great Communities:
A Candid Discussion About
Entrepreneurship and Philanthropy

The greatest idea is the one inside of you—the one great idea of deciding how you will use your business to give back. As your company grows and you are able to take care of yourself and your family, you are faced with the life-changing decision of how you will give back to your local and global community. *What will you do with your life's success?* Who will you help? How will you make life a little better for someone else outside of your family and friends?

Only you can answer these questions, and that is *your* one great idea. For me, I used my company, Financial Voyages LLC, to launch an even greater endeavor, Global Women Entrepreneurs.org, a non-profit organization focused on promoting economic growth through entrepreneurship and philanthropy. This effort was based on my one great idea that "Great Leaders Build Great Communities." As entrepreneurs become more successful, they tend to want to give back. I founded Global Women Entrepreneurs.org to inspire, support, and educate women entrepreneurs on a global front because I believe that women entrepreneurs tend to invest in education and communities.

The Power of the Purse

As a nationally-certified woman-owned company[1], I believe that the world has yet to see the economic power that woman-owned businesses have on local and global communities. In the United States, "Women-owned firms employ nearly thirteen million people and generate $1.9 trillion in sales. [In fact] between 1997 and 2006, majority women-owned firms (51 percent or more women-owned)

---

[1] Women Business Enterprise Council (WBENC) www.wbenc.org and the National Business Owners Corporation (NBOC), www.nboc.org.

grew at twice the rate of all firms (42 percent versus 24 percent)."[2] In Africa, author Malcolm Ray states that "Although the research on African women entrepreneurs is limited, anecdotal evidence supports the belief that women who possess economic means invest more in education, their families, and communities."[3]

Fueling Economic Development through Entrepreneurship

Entrepreneurship fuels economic development in developed and developing countries. There are many reasons women become entrepreneurs. Recent research shows that "in developing countries, women are more likely to turn to entrepreneurship out of economic necessity to supplement family income because employment opportunities are scarce and access to childcare is limited or non-existent. In developed countries, women largely turn to entrepreneurship to capitalize on an opportunity."[4] Regardless of the region of the world, women need the right tools to launch and grow businesses.[5]

In 2007, I was one of the first entrepreneurs in Georgia (United States) to make a presentation in front of the Joint Economic Development Committee. I shared my thoughts on what Georgia was doing well to support small business and areas where improvements could be made. The lessons I walked away with as a result of this experience were: 1) we can make a difference in our community, 2) investing in entrepreneurship is a wise choice and the return on the investment benefits generations, and 3) my grandparents will be even more proud.

Leaders Don't Wait . . . After Careful Consideration . . . They Act

Leaders don't wait. Effective leaders connect with the needs and internalize those needs with what they are passionate about; they assess the risk, and act. This is what happened to me.

Recently I was at a crossroad. I could continue to grow my company and live out my life contributing here and there, but the path of entrepreneurship took me to a new level. Before starting my company, I assessed my current situation. I was in my thirties and earning a capped income. I had limited flexibility in working hours,

[2] The Center for Women's Business Research, Key Facts About Women-Owned Businesses—2007 Update, underwritten by the MassMutual Financial Group, http://www.cfwrb.org.

[3] Malcolm Ray, Africa's Courageous Women Entrepreneurs, Business In Africa online, September 26, 2005, http://icms.iac.iafrica.com.

[4] United Nations Association of the United States and the Business Council for the United Nations, April 29 2003.

[5] Jalbert, Susanne E. 2002. *Women Entrepreneurs in the Global Economy.*

which minimized my ability to pursue other known and undiscovered interests. This did not sit well with me and was definitely not how I wanted to live out the rest of my life.

To enjoy a more flexible lifestyle, financial security, and to contribute something more, I knew that accepting the risk of taking an idea and turning it into products and services was where I would experience real joy. I would *never have* forgiven myself had I let this opportunity pass and if I *had become* a bystander in my own life rather than taking center stage. So I launched my company to transfer specialized knowledge and experience to help clients make insightful decisions.

As the company grew, I realized that I had not given back enough. After years of focusing on my formal education, career, family, and now business, I had not really committed to giving. Entrepreneurship has afforded me a flexible lifestyle and a degree of financial security. Now there were no real barriers to contributing to something bigger than myself. I not only wanted to give more, I needed to give more to live authentically.

This discovery of using my life to make a difference is not new; it has always been inside of me, but nothing has moved me enough to really take action, or at least nothing that I paid attention to because I was busy living my life.

Beyond the Business Lies the One Great Idea

About three years into my business, I asked myself what I wanted to do as my company and I matured. I believe that taking the lessons I have learned in business and sharing them with other emerging businesses on a global scale is the best use of my life. This endeavor is so exciting because I now have a framework in Global Women Entrepreneurs.org where others can contribute and women can display their companies and communities. The combination of entrepreneurship and philanthropy among women demonstrates the economic power that women-owned businesses have on local and global communities.

What You Can Do To Act Globally

We can be change agents in our world in a good way. Giving back looks at the heart and creates an equal playing field because we can all serve.[6] So it really doesn't matter if you are Bill and Melinda Gates or Warren Buffet, Oprah Winfrey, Bono, Bill Clinton, Muhammad Yunus, or the many other public and private philanthropists. You can make a difference in your communities, locally and globally.

---

[6] "Everyone can be great because anyone can serve." Dr. Martin Luther King, Jr.

Giving back is not just good business, but giving back fuels the soul. It is what you do with your success that really matters. At some point in an entrepreneur's life cycle, you will be faced with business and life immortality. You will want to give back in a big way once you realize how your hard work and perseverance has paid off. When you do, consider contributing to a broader community. Build this giving concept into the fabric of your company's strategy because this is your legacy well beyond the wonderful products and services you deliver.

Great Leaders Build Great Communities.

Meet Pamela Robinson...

PAMELA ROBINSON is founder and CEO of Financial Voyages LLC www.teamfv.com, a Business Analysis and Decision Support Solutions Company.

She is also the founder of Global Women Entrepreneurs.org, a non-profit organization focused on promoting economic growth through entrepreneurship and philanthropy.

Pamela Robinson
Financial Voyages LLC
3340 Peachtree Rd., NE, Suite 1800
Atlanta, GA 30326
www.teamfv.com

Philanthropy
www.globalwomenentrepreneurs.org

One Great Idea

16

Maurice Ramirez

One Idea That Can Save Your Life!

After Hurricane Katrina and even after Hurricane Andrew, Arnie Goodman saw people who were absolutely oblivious of even the most basic information about themselves. In some cases the rushing waters even stripped their clothing from their bodies.

They didn't have identification. They didn't have insurance cards. They didn't have insurance papers for liability insurance or for property insurance. They didn't have anything that we in our industrial technology information age think of as identifying a person. At the same time, because he is on the forefront of infrastructure recovery he knew that the technologies existed to provide people with the ability to carry that information with them.

At most of the hospitals in New Orleans there were no medical records other than what people were carrying with patients as they evacuated. The electronic systems were totally lost. Patients would arrive from the community and when asked for their medication list would say, "Ask my pharmacist or call the pharmacy—they know what I take."

The pharmacy was under water. That information was lost forever. These are people who take medicine every day.

With over thirty years of experience in the disaster recovery and infrastructure recovery industry, Arnie Goodman knew there had to be a solution—there was always a solution.

He started out life as a marine, saw two tours of combat and made over 200 jumps in Vietnam; he came back uninjured, won multiple awards while in the service of his country, started a construction firm in Cleveland, Ohio, and through his work in construction became involved in the first infrastructure recovery, building recovery, and ultimately full disaster recovery. He'd been a contractor to the federal government for over twenty years. His business worked on almost a daily basis with entire communities in recovery after a natural disaster or an industrial accident.

Arnie had a vision of a solution so simple and yet so powerful that he sought out the best expert he could find.

He actually tracked me down and traveled to Washington, D.C., where I was giving a speech. He said that he had this idea of putting actual medical records, not just a list of lists, but real medical records on a device that people could wear like a watch or a wristband or a dog tag. It would not be washed off; it would follow them everywhere, and would work no matter what as long as there is a working laptop computer available. When he first approached me he had a non-working prototype. I told him to show me that he could make it work and I'd work with him.

It was about six months into this process and six months later when he came back to me and said, "Okay, we have in place everything except a flow chart—actual knowledge of how to put together the record—and someone who can do the programming. I know what it needs to be; I've talked to the experts. Do you know how to do it?"

I used to be a programmer before medical school, I still have friends in the U.S. Defense industries who are programmers, and I knew people who could give us the level of encryption that was necessary, the level of redundancy, and the change tracking. I had been involved in the early development of electronic medical records back in the 1980s and early '90s, so I knew the basic premise.

In the eighteen months that followed, The original *My Medical Records* software was developed. Now we are ready to give away our "Lite" version.

A Personal Health Record (PHR) is an electronic database that stores your medical records. Most of the personal health records are actually "on line sites," which of course has all of the risks of identify theft that transmitting any highly sensitive personal data on line has with it.

There are a few of the "on line" personal health records that combine transmitting records either by fax or by mail with putting your records "on line" in a password protected form. There was a recent article in *Reader's Digest,* of all places, that reminded consumers that their insurance information is like a credit card with a million-dollar limit. If somebody can impersonate you and if that person requires very expensive health care, you could actually end up responsible, not only for the bill, but without your own health insurance because your health insurance company will drop you.

A Personal Medical Record (PMR), on the other hand, is actually a type of personal health record. A Personal Medical Record is an electronic storage device database that follows you. Most of them exist in USB flash drives. These are little thumb drives that people carry in their pockets or attach to their keys. Some people wear them around their neck. They are also available in watches and wristbands, dog tags, and any number of things. I recently saw one that was part of a bottle opener and another that was part of a Swiss Army Tool.

This is in contrast to an electronic medical record like your doctor or hospital uses. An electronic medical record is a collection of multiple medical records. It's a database that holds information about thousands of patients, very much like the bank can hold information about many accounts. There are also levels of redundancy just like in a bank accounting system. Every change in an Electronic Medical Record (EMR) is recorded permanently and can be traced back to not only who made the change, but at what time and what specific characters—what specific letters—in the record, were changed. If a word is misspelled, entered, and then somebody goes back and just corrects the spelling error, the change is tracked in the Electronic Medical Record.

Personal Health Records do not have that level of security. If you were to make a change in a Personal Health Record, whether through the software or by hacking into the software, little or no footprint is left behind. That of course leads to the opportunity for fraud, error, and just makes the whole system insecure.

In addition to the differences in security, the Personal Health Record is aimed at one person. The ideal would be to have all of the security features of an EMR including encryption, change tracking, the ability for off-sight storage, the ability to have a back-up copy on your own computer, and the ability to synchronize with other electronic medical records in your personal health record.

All electronic medical records should be able to synchronize with central repositories, which are off-sight storage systems that are as secure as a bank. By 2014 every health care provider in the United States will be required by law to have switched over to a fully paperless Electronic Medical Record System.

To be able to synchronize with your Personal Health Record would then mean that you as an individual would have all of your medical records with you at all times.

The Original My Medical Records software is actually both. It's an Electronic Medical Record for one. It's beyond a Personal Health Record because it has tracking and it has encryption. It's not just "password" protected. It would take a halfway decent hacker a half hour to crack most if not all of the personal health records technology out there. A couple of the "on line" ones might be a challenge for about an hour.

The Original My Medical Records has government level encryption. Even if someone gets in around the password, if they don't break the encryption, the most they get is a scrambled file that is useless to them.

No matter what you program, it can be broken, but somebody would have to be truly dedicated for days in order to crack this encryption. If they are that dedicated there are other ways to get your health records that take less effort than breaking into your copy of The Original My Medical Records. The idea is to create something that insures your records are available when you need them.

I'm a scuba diver. During the thirty years I've spent diving I've fortunately never had a serious event—I never got the bends and never had an equipment failure. Last year, in 2006, diving on the Spiegel Grove (a wonderful dive opportunity) in 120 plus feet of water, I had regulator failure. My regulator vented almost my entire tank in a matter of minutes. I was on a dive that would require a decompression stop along the way. I was going to be out of air before I would reach the surface. I was fortunate, even though I was separated from my buddy, another diver made the assent with me and insured I got to the surface safely with my decompression stop—barely.

Had I not been able to do that there would have been a problem. I have a medical history. I now wear a dive watch that has a flash drive and The Original My Medical Records software in it. My entire medical record can go down to 100 meters with me. If I were to ever have an accident, rescuers would be able to plug this into a computer and immediately see my records without any difficulty.

Of course, diving is not the only high-risk sport. I have friends who are competition mountain bikers who now wear a watch or wristband with The Original My Medical Records software for the same reason. If they ever have an accident on their bike and there is nobody around to give their medical history, they'll have their records with them. Even though they are fairly young men with little if any medical problems the medications they take and the few problems they have had will be available. More importantly, there is a way to record every interaction they experience in a health care setting and for these records to travel with them immediately and in a way they control.

The other thing is something called "Patient Safety." In 1999 the Institute of Medicine of the National Academies, a part of our federal government, issued a report called *To Err is Human.* It detailed among other things the inaccuracies in medical records and medication administration. Basically, it reported that correct orders were written and then given to the wrong patient or observations written on the wrong chart, wrong legs being amputated—a left became a right at some point because it was written from a handwritten note into a computer.

A system like this would allow patients' records from their doctors to follow them all the way into the hospital and be verified in the operating room to ensure the correct operation was being performed. If the doctor in the community says that a left leg is diseased and the operation plan indicates that the right leg should be amputated, The Original My Medical Records may be the only thing that stands between the patient and the loss of both legs. Of course there have been challenges in developing such a device.

The biggest challenge is the fact that electronic medical records are actually written to a set of standards. There are two standards out right now. We choose to use the HCL4 standard, which is the predominate standard in the industry. It is the most recently updated and provides a set of protocols and, in some cases, an actual structure that is common across all electronic medical records. The key is the ability to exchange between multiple platforms.

Our second challenge was the fact that we were operating across multiple operating systems. Some hospitals are "Windows" based, while others use UNIX and Lenix. There are even Mac hospitals out there. We had to be able to function across all of these systems. We initially developed in the Java operating system by Sun Micro System because Java has tremendous cross platform interoperability.

The final and most recent challenge for us has been acceptance. Everybody is afraid of "viruses." Everybody is afraid of "spyware." You have to get hospital IT Departments past the fear that plugging into somebody else's Personal Electronic Medical Record is going to somehow infect their hospital system or steal all the data. It isn't a logical argument. Even though you would think that computer technicians and information technology (IT) professionals would be extremely logical people, they're driven by the same fear and the same job self-preservation as most professionals. If there is a threat to that, such as an external device, their initial response is, "We don't want it." That is changing—in time this will be the standard, not just because we're doing it, but because so many others are as well.

We also made The Original My Medical Records capable of maintaining images of non-healthcare documents. There are lists for family members and other emergency contacts, employers, and insurance information. We made these lists unlimited so you can record home insurance and other information if you choose.

The first version of the software was originally developed for two reasons: We needed to determine the feasibility of what we wanted to do. Could it actually be done in a reasonable program size and with the power that we thought was necessary? We also needed to be certain we could emulate all the features that every one of our other competitors had. There are a number of other companies that are producing Personal Health Records. They don't have the power, nor do they have the encryption. They don't even have the synchronization that the full retail version of The Original My Medical Records has. We wanted to be certain that we could provide everything that the competition already offered.

The software developed during the feasibility analysis became our "Lite" version. It was never intended to become a commercial retail product. It was an internal development milepost. When we finished the feasibility studies, it became evident to Arnie that we had something here that people needed in their hands today.

There will be another disaster. We made it through 2006 without any major hurricanes and only a few disasters worldwide. Arnie was absolutely convinced that since we had already spent the money to develop the "Lite" software, it was a waste to dump a lot of electrons in the electronic recycling bin on the computer. He decided that for only a few pennies more we could give it away. We are doing that on our Web site.

The "Lite" version will be very effective for many people. Full encryption is in the "Lite" version so the level of security is no less in the "Lite" version than in the full retail version. The full retail version provides many features that the "Lite" version does not.

The full function version enables such functions as "change tracking," which is functioning in the "Lite" version but is not visible. It cannot be retrieved by the user. In the full version the "change tracking" is retrievable. In the full version, synchronization with a repository, with your physician's office and with your home computer is enabled.

Arnie also designed preloaded hardware/software packages. The Original My Medical Records Software is mated with hardware that is designed to survive in items such as the dive watch I use. The wristbands are waterproof to ten meters. There is a wallet card that was designed in Israel and waterproof to one hundred meters. The wallet card is shock resistant and can be dropped off a nine-story building; it has even survived explosions in Israel. These are pieces of equipment that most people can't get.

The software preloaded is also pre-tested. Everything is ready to go—encryption is in place and all you have to do is enter your data and you are ready to roll.

The hardware choices were based on two things: What would people find innocuous in their regular lives? Watches, elastic wristbands, key fobs, and wallet cards were obvious choices. Watches are ubiquitous and functional parts of both leisure and business wear. Elastic wristbands provide durability and fashion, particularly to the youth market. Key fobs are not ideal for this purpose, but they are popular so we chose the key fob that was rugged enough to survive but functional enough to still use. The wallet card was an obvious choice for those people who just want that discrete form of back-up protection.

All the hardware has "My Medical Records" written on the side. It is a declarative statement. There is no question as to what is contained on that device. All in all, this is one great idea that can save your life.

Meet Dr. Maurice A. Ramirez...

DR. MAURICE A. RAMIREZ is co-founder of *Disaster Life Support of North America, Inc.,* a national provider of Disaster Preparation, Planning, Response, and Recovery education. Through his consulting firm *High Alert, LLC,* he serves on expert panels for pandemic preparedness and health care surge planning with U.S. Congressional and Cabinet members. Board certified in multiple medical specialties, Dr. Ramirez is Founding Chairperson of the *American Board of Disaster Medicine* and serves the nation as a Senior Physician-Federal Medical Officer in the National Disaster Medical System. He was the Chief Medical Officer for *My Medical Records, LLC,* a company dedicated to empowering patients by keeping their medical records with them at all times.

Dr. Maurice Ramirez
1200 Providence Blvd.
Kissimmee, FL 34744
Phone: 866-231-4755
E-mail: renaissancedoc@mauricearamirez.com

My Medical Records, LLC
Attn: Arnold Goodman, CEO
30799 Pinetree Rd.
Pepper Pike, OH 44124
www.TheOriginalMyMedicalRecords.com

17

Lori Wilk

Your Energy Moves Others

Individuals have energy. Groups have energy. Events have energy. Buildings have energy. Businesses have energy. As the energy we are exposed to changes, the way we feel changes too.

Many of us understand the financial aspects of our business more than how to motivate the people inside our company by adjusting energy. If you're already successful with money and logic, you will be more well-rounded if you understand how energy impacts your business and staff.

Energy—personal energy—is powerful and fluid. It is technically invisible to the naked eye, but its results are apparent. We don't see the streams of energy continually flowing from our bodies. We can see and often feel the results of what the energy moves, influences, impacts, changes, helps, or hinders with its presence.

We are human and sometimes we get so busy we forget. Our five senses are a part of us and how we feel effects us and others in our lives.

Before reading this, you might not have taken the time to calculate the energy factors into your corporate profitability, but I'll bet you have noticed days when the energy is off and things don't seem to be going right. You might be wondering, "What's wrong here?" and "How do I fix it?"

In this chapter, I will share with you some of the lessons I have learned in business and parenting using energy to move others. Ignoring energy is like ignoring life—it would be a mistake.

It will be up to you to decide whether you want to accept, reject, or ignore these concepts.

Would you like to be able to move others for better results? What would it mean if you achieved better results with your business and in your personal life?

Do you want to use this invisible power to have a better life? If that is important to you, then read on.

Understanding how energy moves others can help take your business and personal life to new levels of performance, productivity, success, and happiness.

I have to thank the Walt Disney Company for many of the daily messages I heard about creating happiness while working in the field of Disney Entertainment at Walt Disney World in Florida. I owe a tremendous thanks to Worldmark by Wyndham for proving to me that a lifestyle of regular vacationing in high quality resorts totally improves your energy and enthusiasm.

This book was created to take a unique collection of business ideas and to make them available to those learning organizations and professionals who could use these gems of wisdom to be more successful. It is definitely an honor to help others learn more about energy and how to change lives by maximizing its positive forces.

As a motivation speaker and energy practitioner, I use my gifts in

> "Believe in what you do, soon others will too."—Lori Wilk

front of audiences daily and practice expanding the reach of my energy as far as possible as a featured expert author online at http://www.ezinearticles.com and by broadcasting in many forms of media including an Internet talk show called *Successipes.* It features recipes for success in business and living and episodes are available for viewing at http://www.success-talk.com.

I am even using the latest methods of podcasting and online Webinars.

The energy that moves businesses to higher levels of productivity and profitability are strong, constant, and positive.

The energy that moves people the most is authentic and from the heart. When this energy is experienced by individuals or groups of people, they usually feel good. People are desperate to feel good. Too many things make them feel bad.

According to South African Naturalist, Baba Diom, "In the end, we conserve what we love, love what we understand, and understand only what we have been taught." This chapter teaches us that we have the power to reach amazing levels of success by sharing positive energy with those around us and doing it every day.

Each day we have the opportunity in business to move incrementally ahead of our competitors. If we move forward, even a little each day, within a short period of time we will be much further ahead.

You do not win if you don't play. Tony Mowbray of Australia once told me that his greatest fear in life was not getting started. You don't finish what you don't start. Start today by evaluating the energy of the people, places, and things in your surroundings. How to they make you feel?

If positive energy moves people in a positive direction, why doesn't every company have amazing results?

When companies start they tend to have a smaller group of people working there and a strong core belief that fuels their start-up.

Growing businesses involves shifts in energy as people, and often multiple locations, are added to the corporate mix. Not all of the new ingredients are positive. As the business changes, so does the energy of the business.

It is often said that we know what to do, yet we don't do what we know. If we want positive results, we continue adding positive energy flow to our business. The most effective leaders are constant and clear in their communication. New technology offers a variety of methods to keep your messages in front of your staff including podcasts and Webinars.

The fastest destroyers of a company are negative energy and persistent complainers and contaminators. Managers ask me how to handle these types. I recommend immediate action and being clear about your expectations. If you can't get your employees to cooperate, let them find a new place to work. It's easier to eliminate negativity before it destroys the business than to have to start a whole new business.

My personal parenting experience of surviving my son's negative teenage years helped shape my opinions about how to handle negativity. I provided my son daily with positive messages. He wasn't impressed at the time. He was angry every day because he couldn't understand why I insisted on being so positive every day, without fail—no exceptions. He told me many times that life wasn't that good or easy and that happiness was fake.

I stayed constant and offered positive, loving support, every day. Finally he got a job. He made a decision on his first day of employment to have a good attitude and to provide excellent customer service. His new employer was impressed. My son received a raise on his first day of work.

When I heard the good news, I smiled. I finally knew that the energy I shared with Craig made an impact on his life. I had remained positive and constant with my messages even though there were days when I wondered if I had the strength to keep them up. It's amazing how the negativity of people you are around can zap your own energy.

Sometimes we meet a person who is negative about everything. Focus and get on track. Offer positive encouragement even to the most negative of people. Don't give up. Wish them well when they leave.

One man was so mean and negative to me that he felt bad about his attitude and told his wife that he was wrong for being so defensive and negative. He told his wife that he should have paid attention to what I was trying to help him with. A year later, he actually drove two hundred and fifty miles to apologize and let me know that I had helped him change his life for the better. That was uplifting. You don't always know when you've really made someone find a new path in life.

It's easy to slide into a negative mode if you allow all the negative thoughts you are exposed to into your life. It pays to go out of your way to avoid negative energy. To perform at peak levels in business you should eliminate as many negative people, places, or things from your life and add the positives.

Many people ask for suggestions about finding the positive forces. The positive forces can be anything from people to programs that make you smile, laugh, and enjoy. You can find uplifting books, music, programs, events, activities, and even television shows or comedy clubs.

Move your body and get out of a rut if you want your energy to impact others in a positive way. If you've been sitting too much, stand up, take a walk, move to some music, or get out of the building.

If you expect people to have a positive attitude and to be respectful of other co-workers, employees, and customers, it's important to monitor whether your expectations are being met. Your business depends on it. If you are not getting the response you need and the results you want, you have to insist that actions are changed or take action yourself to eliminate the energy problems.

You can replace and train people with positive attitudes who are willing to contribute and add to your company. You can lose your entire company if you allow negative energy to destroy your employee base, your customers, and the bottom-line.

When I have eliminated an employee from the organization because they would not comply with being part of creating a positive work environment, the remaining staff became clear about my determination and intentions with the business.

You have probably encountered coworkers who are depressing to be around. Some of the most depressing are those whose get up and go, has gotten up and left. Worse yet, you don't see signs of their energy coming back any time soon. These people lack energy, enthusiasm, or anything remotely exciting. They give people the impression that they are only on the clock for a paycheck. They are not concerned about their performance or service and they are going through the motions but not doing anything significant. They are physically present but you don't get the impression that they are mentally with you. They are not getting the desired results, others are not impressed, and some employees are trying to figure out how to get rid of them or away from them.

What does it take to win in the business world today with the added pressure created by the addition of online competition in every single industry imaginable?

Businesses will often win by the "incremental edge." Let's call it IE. Do you have it? How are you going to get it?

The incremental edge takes you beyond what your competitors are providing. The over-the-top service you provide to a customer, the extra polite and attentive customer service, and energy can be just what keeps you at the top.

Customers have expectations about how your company will treat them and what they will experience before they enter your business location. If they get what they expected, your results might be good, but it will be nothing so earth-shattering as to make your business their topic of conversation to everyone they meet.

If your energy and the level of excitement about your product is over the top and the customers can feel different after a business encounter with your company and staff, you have a good chance they will use your product or service again and tell others about the positive experience.

As a motivational speaker, when the audience members are going out of their way to talk to you about how your presentation moved them and impacted them before they leave, you know you are using your energy in a way that moves others.

When people are very impressed they tell others. By motivating your staff with your energy you will often find that your most important asset—your employees—become even more valuable to you because they stay with your company longer.

I have often asked executives how they could allow their greatest asset, their employees, whom they've recruited, trained, and developed to be added to the bottom-line of their competitors by making the wrong business moves that cause their employees to quit. If people hate your energy they will quit.

Most companies know the value of a repeat customer. It's powerful when customers can't wait to give you more money and even more powerful when they are recommending you to friends and family because you have moved them to a level of satisfaction they have not expected.

For additional ideas about how to involve energy and your five senses in your business, go to http://www.loriwilkarticles.com. If you want to be able to measure the results of your energy to move others into action you will have to evaluate how you are using your energy. Do you create positive, uplifting, energetic experiences in your work environment on a daily basis like a good habit? How would your customers, friends, and family rate your flow of energy?

If your energy is going to move others to positive results such a employee retention, lower absenteeism, higher productivity, greater sales, more money and profits on the bottom-line, you should have a warm, inviting energy. If your energy invites others, they will want what you have, they will want to stay, they will be receptive to spending more money with you, they will want more of what you and your company can offer, and they will send others to be a part of what you can provide.

Your energy either moves people toward you and your business or it will repel them from you. Guess who will be making more money and ultimately be much happier?

Positive energy will attract more people to your business and will help you keep the doors open. If the doors are open, it's much easier to pay the bills and keep going.

It's easier to expand your business when more of your customers feel moved and uplifted with your business than it is if your customers are annoyed. Negative experiences are discussed much more frequently than customers than good experiences. I am sure you can remember a day when someone called you and said," You won't believe what happened today . . ."

Positive energy moves quickly and spreads to others. To impact your business, respond quickly to any changes in the energy in your environment. Don't wait; take action. If the energy is fabulous, capitalize on it. If there's something wrong, fix it.

"Patience is for those who are willing to wait. I'm not waiting."
—Lori Wilk
"Any time is a great time to shine."
—Lori Wilk
"If they are going to listen, make sure you've got something good to say."
—Lori Wilk

Here are six ways to adjust energy:
1. Take a vacation. Change your scenery. Go to a place you have never been before or a place you have not been in a long time.

See the world and anything about your life from a different point of view.

2. Wear different clothing. You can adjust your colors to feel and project a different image. Your clothing and how you look and feel wearing different clothing sends out a variety of messages. Most women get excited about the thought of shopping to have something new to wear.

3. Move your body. Shake up your energy or just get it to flow. For some people, circulation is all they need to improve their energy. For others, a vigorous workout is necessary. You might want to take a walk, hit some golf balls, go bowling, pump iron, get in the ocean or a pool, take a Jacuzzi, get on a treadmill, or make love.

4. Change what you hear. Get some different sounds in your head, mind, or near your body. You can change your radio station, television channels, buy a new CD or DVD, or go to a place where you'll have a different conversation than your usual routine. Find new sounds. You might want to add sounds or get quiet—you know if you need more or less sound to adjust your energy.

5. Eat something different. Get some unique tastes, spices, and flavors flowing in your system. Stimulate different moods or feelings with food. It will give you something else to talk about tomorrow. People love to talk about eating.

6. Adjust your temperature. If you've been in an environment that has been very hot and humid, maybe you just need to cool off a bit and get refreshed. If your environment has been very dry, maybe you need to get near water to adjust your energy. If you have been on level or flat environments, consider a change in elevation.

I am looking forward to meeting and working with many of you soon. I wish you good luck, great business, and wonderful energy.

Meet Lori Wilk...

Lori Wilk was born in New York. She began her television career at CBS-TV at age ten. She later created, produced, and hosted NEA approved KID's TV which airs to eighteen million viewers daily. Lori has worked with major corporations including Eastern Airlines, Walt Disney World Company, Cendant, and Hilton. As an award-winning motivational speaker, trainer, and author she has helped corporations and individuals in thirty-five states, the Caribbean, and UK. Lori's Internet talk show called Successipes: Recipes for Success in Business and Living is now being pod cast from http://www.success-talk.com. Lori is the author of Without Me You'll Be Eating Out of Garbage Cans, Trash to Cash Toolkit, and is now working with Insight Publishing on Now Would Be Fine, The Magic of Momentum, and 90-Minute Selling. Her corporate clients have included NASA, IBM, ADP, Tico Financial Corp, various branches of the United States Military, many U.S. cities. She currently works with Wyndham Worldwide.

Lori Wilk
P.O. Box 531344
Henderson, NV 89053
Phone: 702.270.0622
E-mail: Speakupinc@yahoo.com
www.loriwilk.com

18

Recently, our firm, ROI Training & Consulting (ROI), made a presentation to a company interested in determining the feasibility of an expansion project.

We met in the client's custom-designed corporate boardroom. The CEO sat at the head of the large, rectangular, mahogany conference table. His seven-person leadership team settled into their high-backed leather chairs around the table.

Following perfunctory introductions, the meeting began. Our ROI team was well prepared. We had our reference material readily available and we maximized the room's state-of-the-art audio-visual equipment. From the engaging interaction with the team members, it appeared they were fully involved.

Everything progressed according to plan.

About fifteen minutes into our presentation, the CEO, who had said very little until this point, took off his glasses, leaned forward in his chair, and in a very authoritarian voice said, "Annarose and Charles, if I asked you to identify the single most important benefit of being a husband and wife team working together as equal business partners or copreneurs, what would you say?"

Wow! Talk about getting thrown a curve ball! We had no PowerPoint presentation, matrix, or handout to address *that* issue. Yet, as if the question had been the next item on the agenda, the response came quickly, "Being able to work on our marriage while we are at work."

The CEO looked pleased that we were able to think on our feet. He sat back in his chair, stretched his right arm toward us, used his eyeglasses as a pointer, smiled, nodded, and declared, "Now, *that* is one great idea!"

Here is the rest of the conversation:

CEO: Charles, Annarose, you do know that most husbands and wives do not work together professionally, so what exactly do you mean by "working on your marriage at work"?

Charles: Although copreneurship is the fastest growing segment of family-based businesses, we are aware that most married couples have separate careers. What we mean by working on our marriage at work is basic. It simply means that the skills Annarose and I use in the workplace to build successful business relationships are the same skills we use to build our successful personal relationship.

CEO: Do you mean you interact with your clients in the office the same way you interact with each other at home?

Annarose: Obviously there is a difference with how we interact with our clients and how we interact with each other at home. At home there is much less formality. Yet the skills, especially the interpersonal skills we use on a daily basis, are the same. Creating a successful marriage is no accident.

CEO: And creating a successful business is no accident.

Charles: Both take planning.

CEO: As a businessman I know the value of planning. After all, it is the reason my team is meeting with you today.

Charles: Of course in and out of the workplace it is vital to know how to plan and look ahead. And when we plan we often work as a team.

CEO: Yes, teamwork is an invaluable tool to manage our business. We put a lot of time, effort, and focus into strengthening our work teams so our business prospers.

Annarose: Sometimes our personal team relationships become less of a priority and we may forget to set aside time to spend together to plan, talk, or play together.

CEO: I know at work we often eat lunch together, which helps us get to know each other. Outside the office, I wonder how many of my staff dine with their families on a regular basis?

Charles: Good question.

Annarose: And you need certain skills to cultivate relationships.

CEO: My leadership team is living proof successful relationships take skill.

(The leadership team glanced at each other with tight-lipped smiles as if they were sharing an inside joke.)

CEO: These men and women have varied backgrounds, experiences, personalities, and talents. In our team relationship, we share our points of view and remain open to different perspectives.

Annarose: So you value their opinions?

CEO: Sure—their diversity is a powerful business tool.

Charles: By respecting their opinions, even if you do not necessarily agree, you show you are willing to learn from each other and capitalize on the diversity. Respect is key to any relationship.

CEO: Leaders and employees who respect each other build high performing teams. Companies that respect their customers build profitable businesses. And so, families who respect each other prosper—together.

Annarose: Well stated. And there are very simple ways to show respect.

CEO: In the office I regularly thank my employees for doing their jobs and customers for giving us their business. Expressing appreciation is a sign of respect and it tells the other person he or she is valued.

Annarose: How about at home?

CEO: I confess, I don't say "thank you" as often as I should at home.

Charles: In our workplace valuing different opinions, appreciating efforts, and demonstrating respect are routine expectations.

CEO: You are right. Respect is key. I truly respect my leadership team. If I did not, I definitely would not want to hear what they had to say, especially when they question some of my decisions.

Charles: You make a good point. No one likes to be criticized. Accepting feedback is often difficult. However, we know it is vital to be able to give and accept feedback in order to propel our performance so we can be the best we can.

CEO: Yes, leaders, co-workers, friends, and even spouses all need to be able to give and receive constructive feedback.

Annarose: That is true. And in order to give feedback, we need to have strong communication skills.

CEO: We all know how vital effective communication is to running a successful business. And now that we are talking, I realize that effective communication is also important at home.

Annarose: Tell me, at work, what do you do when you want to make sure your staff or your customers understand your message?

CEO: That's easy. I use a lot of different techniques to make sure they understand what I have to say.

Annarose: Do you know what you are talking about before you start talking? Do you choose your words wisely? Do you use an appropriate tone of voice? Do you make eye contact? Do you link your body language with your words and tone? Do you make sure it is the right time and place to have a conversation?

CEO: Okay, okay—stop there, I get it. And the answer is "Yes" to every single question. Being able to effectively communicate is a skill I practice and have developed over time. And that is why I am the boss.

(At this point the CEO and his leadership team enjoyed a meaningful laugh.)

Charles: Now let me ask you: do you practice the same skills at home?

CEO: Hmm, yes. Uh, no. I try, sometimes. I guess life would be greatly improved at home if I did do all those things. I just assume my family can "read" me and they know what I am talking about. Come to think of it, I never thought to transfer the techniques I use at the office to home in order to get my message understood clearly.

Annarose: How about listening—are you a good listener?

(Hearing the question, the leadership team nodded in unison and again shared a low laugh.)

CEO: Yes, I do consider myself a good listener. Listening is difficult. I work hard at it. I don't interrupt others when they are speaking. I ask questions to make sure I understand what is being said. I make eye contact. And I use a litany of other effective techniques so I can make sure I get the message and get it right. If I don't listen, it can cost me a customer or otherwise derail the company. I cannot afford to do that.

Annarose: How about at home? Do you put the same effort into listening as you do at work?

CEO: Ouch, that hurts. I have to admit, when I am at home I don't always listen as well as I know how. I find myself "tuning out" at times.

Charles: Listening is a really hard skill to master and practice all the time. Being in business, we know the true value of listening to our staff and our customers. We also know how good it feels when other people actively listen to us. Off the job, listening is just as vital.

Annarose: And if we fail to effectively listen and communicate, misunderstandings are bound to happen. We all know that misunderstandings are a normal part of everyone's life. It is how we handle misunderstandings that keep minor disagreements from turning into major conflicts.

Charles: Being able to defuse disagreements before they blow into something destructive takes know-how.

Annarose: How do you handle a dissatisfied customer who complains?

CEO: I ask questions, listen, take the time to work through the problem, and resolve the conflict with the customer. I would be out of business if I did not.

Charles: I'll bet you would not ignore your customer, raise your voice, or use inappropriate language.

CEO: Definitely not.

Annarose: And at home we should act the same way. Being able to effectively resolve conflict builds relationships. Conflict resolution is a skill and it takes practice.

CEO: So let me see if I get this. The best thing about working together is being able to "work on your marriage at work." Successful businesses and marriages are no accident—both take planning and teamwork. The interpersonal skills necessary to build successful business relationships are the same skills needed to enhance personal relationships and vice versa. That means we need to practice respect and hone a variety of skills including giving and receiving feedback, effective communication, listening, and conflict resolution, to name a few. Transferring these skills from the work front to the home front means that you indeed are working on your marriage at work.

(There was a short pause. And then, "Eureka!")

CEO: I'll bet an employee who has a healthy personal relationship is a more satisfied and productive employee!

(There was another short pause. The leadership team sat quietly looking at the CEO, seemingly trying to anticipate what he would say next.)

CEO: Let's discuss the feasibility of expanding our employee development program so we can assist everyone in the company to work on their marriage at work.

Annarose and Charles: Now *that* is One Great Idea!

Meet Annarose Ingarra-Milch and Charles Milch...

Copreneurs ANNAROSE INGARRA-MILCH AND CHARLES MILCH own ROI Training & Consulting. They are nationally recognized speakers, facilitators, coaches, authors, and management consultants. Praised by clients and aptly nicknamed, "Mr. and Mrs. Team," this inspiring couple does more than talk about the importance of teamwork and building successful relationships—they live it!

With over fifty years of combined corporate experience—Charles as a CEO in the health and service industry and Annarose as a businesswoman and corporate trainer—these business and life partners tap their synergetic relationship and natural dual perspective to help their clients strengthen workforce, workplace, and work systems relationships. Their impressive list of clients cross industry sectors and range in size from the federal government to independent sole proprietors.

Annarose Ingarra-Milch and Charles Milch
ROI Training & Consulting
1855 Alsace Road
Reading, PA 19604
Phone: 610.378.9499
E-mail: roi-aim@msn.com
www.theconsultantsforum.com/roi.htm

One Great Idea